being a

in a **CRUISE SHIP** world

Written by Steve Elzinga

Cover Design by Steve Elzinga
Edited by Claudia Elzinga
Printed in the USA, April 15, 2012

CONTENTS

PREFACE
Being Saved

This is a book about lifeboats, rescue attempts, salvation—being saved. For many years in the church world, the notion of "being saved" as a concept was well accepted. Heaven and Hell were real. Every human being that ever lived would end up in one of these two places. Those bound for Heaven were saved. The saved were then commissioned to be used by God to help save those who were not saved. Even those who did not go to church understood that they were potentially not saved. And they were sort of okay with that. If a non-churched person was touched by a message by Billy Graham at one of his crusades that person didn't mind going up front to "get saved"—meaning this non-churched person didn't mind considering himself unsaved before walking up.

Today non-churched people don't like to be called unsaved. "What gives you the right to judge me?" they ask. Not only do non-churched people not like to be called unsaved, they don't think it is fair for others, namely anyone trying to save them, to decide what it would mean for them to be saved. I have been a church planter—reaching people that previously did not go to church—for most of my career. I have learned to be very sensitive about how I think about these folks and especially what I call them. In my first church plant I called them "seekers" but eventually I learned not call them anything. My strategy was to just let them know that if they wanted a relationship with God, I would be willing to help them. I tend to think of "saving people," at least for my part in it, as helping people begin and maintain a daily walk with God. Of course, with this definition of "being saved" there are a lot of churched people that still need saving.

As you can see this topic of "being saved" is fraught with many pitfalls. In just two paragraphs of the preface I have probably already offended both non-churched and some churched people. But then this book is not direct-ed at the unsaved, whether churched or non-churched. Neither will ever read it. I have written this book for those who consider themselves to be saved. I am trying to motivate the saved to care for the unsaved.

But this last sentence raises another problem. There are some people, these days, who I would consider to be "saved" who don't like the concept of saved or unsaved. There are popular authors today who are questioning or at least refashioning this notion of being saved. Some au-thors have suggested that Hell is not necessarily an actual place, but more like a concept—that it is at the very least, not eternal. And if there is no Hell, what is there to be saved from?

In the past it was widely accepted that scripture was pretty clear about who was saved and who was not. But now it seems there are many different opinions about how clear Scripture is on this matter.

Then there is the question of what it exactly means to be saved in the first place. Is "being saved" the pre-cise moment where God's grace and a person's conviction meet? Or is "being saved" more of a process—that God has been working His salvation in a person through vari-ous means and people over a long period of time?

Confused? Me too. Personally I tend to see people as being on a continuum. On one end of the continuum there is absolute unbelief. On the other there is belief—knowing God face to face—perfect faith. Then there is every thing in between. Somewhere on this continuum between absolute unbelief and perfect faith, a person crosses over from unbelief to what we call saving faith. Saving faith is not perfect faith. Saving faith is not unbelief. It is somewhere in between.

The question is: How much faith does one need in order for it to count as saving faith? It would appear that a little faith is enough. Jesus often spoke of his disciples as ones with "little faith." They had little faith but we assume they still had saving faith.

How far along the continuum does one need to go to have saving faith? The thief on the cross next to Jesus hardly made any kind of confession and yet he somehow, we presume, had saving faith.

I know many Christians are really concerned about and think they know exactly when unbelief becomes saving faith. And maybe they do. But I've never much concerned myself with the precise moment when faith becomes saving faith. I tend to leave that concern to God. My interest has always been to try to be of some influence to help move every person I meet, in church or outside church, to a closer connection to God. And unlike a lot of modern authors, I do believe in a literal Hell from which every person, including me, needs to be rescued. I believe people are lost and need to be found. I believe that people are drowning is a sea of despair and need saving. And I am convinced that starting, or renewing, or continuing a relationship with God is the way to be rescued, found, and saved.

Saving people. Helping people get a life-giving daily walk with God—perhaps it is an old-fashioned idea. Fine. Then I am old-fashioned. I think people need to be saved. And my part in the unsaved/saving equation is to try and help people begin or continue a relationship with God. And the best way I know how to help people begin or continue in a relationship to God is to connect them to Church—the lifeboat. This is what I can do. This is my part. And God will do His part—the saving part.

Questions:
1. How do you think some of the non-churched people you know would react if they knew you wanted to "save" them?
2. What do you think saving faith is? How would you know if someone has it or not?
3. What concept or point struck you the most as you read this preface?

CHAPTER ONE
The Lifeboats

Noah was six hundred years old when the floodwaters came on the earth. And Noah and his sons and his wife and his sons' wives entered the ark to escape (to be saved from) the waters of the flood.

Genesis 6:6,7

She was seven years old when it happened. Shivering in Lifeboat No. 14, looking across a calm sea, against the backdrop of a million stars, so bright, so clear you could almost reach out and touch them, she watched in utter disbelief as the *Titanic*, the largest ship ever built at the time, slid out of sight. Her name was Eva Hart and she clearly remembered opening her lips in a silent scream of terror.

"The air temperature was freezing and the water temperature not much above that, and from somewhere in the outer darkness, out of the lungs of the hundreds of men and women and children still alive in the freezing ocean, came a chorus of moans and howls, a collective explosion of breath that was a horror to all who heard it. Eva did not know it at the time—the realization would come later when she was older—but one of the screams, must have come from her drowning father."[1]

She last saw him in his dark overcoat, standing at the railing looking down into her lifeboat. She remembered that he leaned over and said, "Be a good girl and hold onto Mommy's hand."

Eva recalled: "I had an enormous teddy bear my father had bought for me the Christmas before we went away. It was almost as tall as I was. I loved it and I used

---

1. I first got interested in the Titanic reading a storybook about it to my kids back in the early '90s. I loved how the author wrote this paragraph as you see it here. I have since lost the book and I have never been able to find it. If someone knows what book this is from, let me know.

to play with it on the deck with my father, and the captain stopped several times and commented on my teddy bear and spoke to my father, who was delighted with him. He was an awfully nice man. I wanted to go back for my teddy bear when my father was carrying me out of the cabin to take me up to the boat deck. I remember saying, 'I want my teddy bear!' He didn't say anything; he just continued to carry me.

> I never had another teddy bear…
> I never wanted another one."

Eva Hart summarizes the whole experience this way:
    "A calm sea,
            a starlit night,
and two and a half hours from the time of impact
    to the time she sank…
                    plenty of time
                to save everyone,
            if only we had enough…lifeboats."

The *Titanic* was the largest movable object in the world at that time. It was built by a workforce of 17,000. It was the ultimate in turn-of-the-century design and technology. The first-class suites cost $75,000 in today's dollars. It was considered virtually unsinkable because of water-tight compartments. It carried 2,227 passengers on its maiden voyage from England to New York.

It had enough lifeboats for only 1,200 passengers.

All 2,227 passengers could have been saved if there had been enough lifeboats. Tragic. Inexcusable. Frustrating. Even 100 years later the lack of lifeboats still elicits a strong reaction.

Why weren't there enough lifeboats?

There is more. You would think that if you were short on lifeboats you would at least fill up the ones you have. When the *Titanic* went down there were only enough lifeboats for a little more than half the people. That means 1,200 could have been saved, and 1,000 would be lost. But, only 700 were saved. Which means there were 500 empty seats in the lifeboats.

Think this through. Not enough lifeboats and yet seats were empty???

Men, women, and children—1,500 total—drowned in the icy waters—500 of them because they did not fill an empty seat in a lifeboat!

Why weren't all the seats filled?

It has been a long hard day. No, it has been a long hard year. Fact is, it has been a long hard century. Every day, for the past 100 years, up at five, working till sundown. Every day, same old thing. Every day, people (neighbors, friends, visitors) wondering what the point is. You wonder sometimes yourself. Maybe the occasional cloud in the sky is enough to keep you going.

Building a boat. A big boat. The largest movable object anyone has ever seen. Your world is in sad shape. God is a patient God but even His patience has run out. There is going to be a big flood. You have been chosen—you and your family—to be saved in a large lifeboat—450 feet long, 75 feet wide and 45 feet high. Through this lifeboat the world will be saved.

Why did God choose you? Who knows. Why does God bother saving anyone at all? When the rain starts coming down...hard, you are not going to argue about it—you get in the boat.

It was God's grace that saved Noah and the generations that followed. Grace was the reason, but the Ark was the means to connect people to the grace. A floating zoo was God's means—His tool to save a world that was going down the drain. The Ark lifeboat was God's way of introducing the whole idea of "being saved"—a theme that the Bible carries all the way through to the coming of God's Son, Jesus Christ.

In Jesus we see how God's grace works. God is a righteous and just God. If God were to let evil triumph, if God were to let injustice prevail, if God were to let sin go unanswered, what kind of God would God be? God's justice requires a reckoning. Wrong must be righted. Someone has to pay when debts are incurred. Who would follow an unjust God?

Humanity freely chose to walk away from God. Justice demands that humanity receive its just reward: death. But God is not only a God of justice, He is a God of love. In Jesus we see the mystery of Grace—the crossroads of God's justice and love. Jesus, the incarnation, the visible manifestation of God's love, the God who becomes a man, demonstrated that love by dying on the cross and thus paying the debt owed by humanity and satisfying God's justice.

Jesus is what is behind God's grace. So far so good. But by what means does God get the grace to us? In Noah's day it was a lifeboat called the Ark. In our day God chooses to use a lifeboat called the Church.

———————

In '87, I moved with my wife Marie and three young sons to Surrey, British Columbia, Canada to plant a new church. Exciting! Scary! With a population of 280,000 and 10-year projections of another 230,000, Surrey would soon outnumber its neighboring city—Vancouver. Bottom line—lots of people live in Surrey.

Before starting the church I wanted to find out just what the need was for one. Here is what I learned: If all the churches in my new city were filled to capacity, only 20,000 people living in Surrey would be able to go to church in their own city on any given Sunday. Translation—210,000 people that lived in Surrey would not be able to go to church in their own community even if they wanted to. Why not? Not enough churches.

Maybe Surrey is somewhat extreme. What is the church situation in the average community in North America? According Robert Logan, long time church planting consultant, 70 percent of North Americans do not have a meaningful church relationship. If you

Google "churches in decline" you will discover that most church leaders believe some 80 to 90 percent of churches have plateaued or are in decline. You will also learn that only two percent of churches are actually reaching the lost. It would seem we do not have enough churches to accommodate the need and certainly not lifeboat churches. Tragic. Inexcusable. Frustrating.

Why aren't there enough lifeboat churches?

There is more. You'd think that if you were short on churches you would at least fill the ones you have. As I attended different churches in my city, I discovered that many of them were half empty.

Think this through. Not enough lifeboats and yet seats are empty??? Men, women, and children—thousands of them—drowning in the icy waters of despair, loneliness, and grief because they do not fill the empty seats in a church!

Why aren't we filling all the seats?

As you look around your own city, you might believe things are not that bad, church wise. Maybe your city seems to have a church on every corner. "Plenty of churches for people to go to in my community!" you say.

In 1912, on the docks of Southampton, England, as 2,227 passengers and crew walked up the gangplank of the *Titanic*, some must have looked up. If they did, they would have seen a whole row of bright, new, ready-to-launch lifeboats. Most of the ill-fated passengers never dreamed that there were only enough lifeboats for half the people on board. What sense would that make? As things turned out somebody should have checked on the

7

lifeboat situation before the *Titanic* hit an iceberg.

In most cities throughout North America, including yours, there aren't enough churches. If you don't believe me, go out and count them. Find out how many people each church in your city holds and then compare with the population of your city. I think you will be surprised to learn how short your community is of churches.

Let's just say that I am right. Maybe your community does not have enough churches to accommodate everyone, but at least your lifeboat, your church is full. Is it?

In 1912, on April 15, at the first sunlight on the morning after the *Titanic* went down, when the rescue ship *Carpathia* steamed into an area of floating debris from the demise of the great sunken ship, 20 lifeboat loads of people were saved—731 people out of 2,227. No one on both sides of the Atlantic could believe that there could have been empty, unfilled seats in the lifeboats. Why wouldn't the lifeboats be filled to capacity? Yet when all the survivors were counted and the total seats tallied up, there were 500 lifeboat seats that went unoccupied.

Your church may not be as full as you think it is. Check your church's capacity and count the number of bodies present in your church service. Is every seat occupied?

Perhaps in your church every seat is occupied. That is great. But if we are ever going to come close to reaching everyone that needs "saving" in each of our communities we are going to have to fill up every church twice. So, if we assume that church buildings could easily accommodate two Sunday morning services, then churches that have only one full service are in reality half empty.

Of course in the end it doesn't really matter how full your church is. What matters is that your church is doing what lifeboats should do—saving people. As I mentioned, only two percent of churches are actually reaching new people for Christ.

Why aren't there enough lifeboat churches?
Why aren't we filling up all the seats?

These are the two questions prompting Part One and Two of this book. We will spend time together trying to get a handle on why thing are the way they are. In Part Three we will be asking these questions in a more positive way: How can we plant more lifeboat churches? How can you and I and the churches we belong to be more effective in being used by God to fill the empty seats next to us? It will require courage to take a good hard look at the church. It will take boldness to take a good hard look into the mirror of our own hearts. And it will take both courage and boldness to step out in faith and be the hands and feet that God uses to rescue people.

The tendency, when looking at topics like "saving the unsaved" is to get defensive. No one likes to think or admit they are not doing all they can to share the Good News of Jesus Christ with others. After all it was God's grace that saved us. How can we turn away from those not yet in our boats?

There is a lot of guilt out in the Christian world over this issue because no matter how you want to rationalize things, when you look at the numbers, the truth is Christians aren't doing a very good job of helping the lost find the church.

Let's stop living in denial about how church growth is really going in North American Churches.

Many did not survive the *Titanic* tragedy because they refused to face the reality of the situation. "How could the unsinkable sink?" There is a greater tragedy taking place right now: billions of people floundering in the ocean of life without a Savior; thousands of people wallowing in the back waters of your city; at least one person you know going down for the third and final count. Let's, by the power of the risen Lord, hear both the call of the Lord and the person in the water, and do something about it.

Questions:

1. What got your attention in this chapter and what might God be trying to say to you through it?
2. What was your reaction when you learned that the *Titanic* did not have enough lifeboats to accommodate its passengers?
3. What was your reaction when you learned that even though there were not enough lifeboats there were still 500 empty seats?
4. What are your thoughts about the church being the prime means to God's grace for people that need it?
5. At this point in the book what do you think of the idea that there is a shortage of churches in North America?
6. Why do you think there are so many empty seats in churches? What is holding you back from filling one?

PART ONE
Why Aren't We Filling All the Seats?

CHAPTER TWO
A Drowning World

*The Lord saw how great man's wickedness on the
earth had become, and that every inclination
of the thoughts of his heart was only evil all the
time. The Lord was grieved that he had made
man on the earth, and his heart was filled with
pain. So the Lord said, "I will wipe mankind,
whom I have created, from the face of the
earth—men and animals, and creatures that
move along the ground, and birds of the air—for
I am grieved that I have made them." But Noah
found favor in the eyes of the Lord.*

Genesis 6:5-8

A few thousand years ago, in the days of Noah, the world was in deep trouble—in need of a lifeboat.

Things haven't changed much.

———————

His name was Timothy O'Brian. Question: Why did he do it? Maybe he needed saving financially and had nowhere to turn. Maybe it was just too much to bear—the guilt he must have felt for letting down a close friend. Maybe the irony of the whole situation convinced him that nothing in his life would ever go right. Maybe missing out on the biggest life ring that he had ever had the chance to grab hold of took the life right out of him. Maybe he thought that if he couldn't save himself, he could at least save his family.

We just don't know why he did it.

You see, Timothy O'Brian and a gambling partner invested money together in a new national lottery in England. Every week, without fail, O'Brian would select the same numbers and purchase a lottery ticket for himself and his partner. Most lottery players get hooked because they settle on a favorite number. Soon they can't NOT pick that number. They neurotically believe that the chances of their number coming up would be greater if they forget to buy one. The true lottery player's worst nightmare is that his number will come up the week he forgets to buy his ticket.

Well, according to my local paper (while I was living in Surrey) this lottery nightmare became a reality for Timothy O'Brian and his gambling partner. Their number came up. O'Brian had forgotten to buy the weekly ticket. He blew their chance to win four million dollars.

So Timothy O'Brian killed himself.

Who is going to save him now? Who is going to save his wife? Who is going to save his family?

———

Her name was Melanie. She grew up not far from my house in Surrey. She went to school, graduated, got a job at a tanning salon—not a career, just a part time job to pay some of the bills. Cute as a kid, she grew up to be a beautiful woman—on the inside as well as the outside.

I first heard her name on the news. She was missing. Someone had abducted her—in broad daylight—from the tanning salon. Our community was shocked.

The next day there was a break in the case. An unknown man had used her bankcard and the police had a couple of computer images of him from the ATM. Who was he? Did he abduct Melanie? Was she still alive? Melanie's dad spoke to all of Canada on TV offering money to whomever had taken his little girl. It was hard not to hurt with him. It was hard not to hope with him.

Days went by. More pleadings. Possible sightings. Hope and fear growing by the day. Nothing tangible.

Two weeks of torture. Then a car was found in an abandoned garage. Inside was the man who had used Melanie's bankcard—dead of an apparent suicide. But where was Melanie? No one knew. No one but the dead man. Where does hope go at a time like this?

It holds on.

But four days later hope died. Melanie's lifeless body was found, in a wooded area just outside a city ironically called "Hope"—in a sleeping bag—naked and cold. That is how we felt, too.

We live in a world in need of a Savior.

———————

It was a chance meeting from the human point of view. My ministry partner Henry Reyenga and I were in California on a whirlwind tour, leading seminars on a new paradigm in discipling. Oh, you haven't heard of it? You will. We broke for lunch, but got separated from the rest of the group so we stopped at the first restaurant we saw. Chinese. It was busy. There wasn't a single table free. But an old man graciously allowed us to sit with him.

Leo. Leo from Reno.

We only had a half hour. We got to the point with Leo. "What is your spiritual dream, Leo?" Henry asked after swallowing his bean curd and rice.

"Well, I tell you boys, I just want to be happy and help my fellow man."

"How about after you die?"

"Well, I'm not sure about that one. I guess I'm just hoping for the best."

Leo is from Czechoslovakia. He came with his parents. He was raised in the church but hated it. He still seemed quite bitter about it.

We told him that we help people grow spiritually. He liked that.

We only had a half hour. He gave us his card. He invited us to come to Reno—stay in his house—anytime. "Just give me a weeks notice, will you?"

We only knew Leo for a half hour. He gave us his heart. He gave us his home. He gave us his business card. I have it in my hand right now.

Leo, from Reno. His hand reaching out. How many Leo's are all around us?

All the lifeboats have been launched. All of them. As the oars glide through the dark, ice cold water, each boat silently, little by little, slips away from the crippled ship, *Titanic*. Though it is a still, moonless night, the ship's lights expose to all on the lifeboats her last moments. They see the bow sink, slowly. They notice the angle of decent becoming steeper. The ships three giant propellers gradually rise out of the water. It is an eerie sight. Some still cannot believe that something as big and new as the *Titanic* could possibly go down. Huddled passengers line the decks, staring at the water as it slowly makes its way over the bow.

There is a commotion on the listing ship. The third class passengers have just arrived from below decks. They have been waiting and wandering about in the bowels of the ship for over an hour. There are no lifeboats for

them. The faces of fathers and mothers reveal to sons and daughters the swell of horror surging from deep within them. They are going…down. There is nothing they can do about it. And they know it.

From the safety of the lifeboat, huddled, cold passengers watch as 1,500 people clamor, climb, and claw their way to the back of the ship—now over a hundred feet in the air. The angle of the deck is growing so steep, people—young and old, rich and poor—stumble and slide toward the approaching water. Objects descend from the stern. With horror, lifeboat passengers realize that the falling objects are people.

Walter Lord, in his book, *A Night to Remember*, describes *Titanic*'s last moments:

> Seen and unseen, the great and the unknown tumbled together in a writhing heap as the bow plunged deeper and stern rose higher. The lights went out, flashed on again, went out for good. A single kerosene lantern still flickered high in the after mast.

> The muffled thuds and tinkle of breaking glass grew louder. A steady roar thundered across the water as everything movable broke lose…29 boilers…tons of coal…15,000 bottles of ale and stout…huge anchor chains (each link weighed 175 pounds)…30 cases of golf clubs and tennis rackets for A.G. Spaulding…5 grand pianos…

> As the tilt grew steeper, the forward funnel toppled over. It struck the water on the starboard side with a shower of sparks and a crash heard

above the general uproar…

The *Titanic* was now absolutely perpendicular. From the third funnel aft, she stuck straight up in the air, her three dripping propellers glistening in the darkness…

Out in the boats, they could hardly believe their eyes. For over two hours they had watched, hoping against hope, as the *Titanic* sank lower and lower. When the water reached her red and green running light, they knew the end was near…but nobody dreamed it would be like this—unearthly din, the black hull hanging at 90 degrees, the Christmas card backdrop of brilliant stars. Some didn't watch. In Collapsible Boat C, Bruce Ismay, President of the White Star Line that owned the *Titanic*, bent low over his oar—he couldn't bear to see her go down. In Boat 1, C. E. Henry Stengle turned his back: "I cannot look any longer…"

Then it happened. Many eyewitnesses gave conflicting reports, but since the 1986 discovery of the *Titanic* on the ocean floor, the reports given have been verified. The stress inflicted on the ship with its bow so far out of the water caused it to break in half. The noise was deafening. Two minutes passed and the *Titanic* settled back slightly to the stern. Then very slowly she slid out of sight.

Silence…

"She's gone; that is the last of her," someone said to Reginald Lee in Lifeboat No. 13.

The silence must have been deafening. For two hours there had been the noise of steam blasting from the funnels. Toward the end, everything crashed and fell to the bow. The largest ship in the world ripped apart with an explosion of steel. Now, there was only the sound of oars cutting through the water.

But soon those in the lifeboats heard a new, unsettling sound—not the sounds of a ship dying violently. It was the sound of people—1,500 of them—trying to catch their breath in the icy water—hundreds of swimmers thrashing in the water, clinging to the wreckage and to each other—desperately calling for help.

The water was 31 degrees Fahrenheit. If they are not rescued within a half hour they will all die.

Do you hear their cries? …their moans? …their desperate pleas? Do you see them reaching out for life? Do you feel their lives slowly drifting away? Do you understand how little time they have left? As you sit in the lifeboat, as you sit every week in your church praying and singing to a gracious life-saving God, do you see and hear those who are drowning? I think you do.

They live next door to you. They work with you. They sit in the stands with you while your kids play sports together. They shop in the same grocery store you do. They often pitch their tent or park their RV next to you at the campground. They enjoy the same crafts and recreational activities as you. Men, women, and children drowning in a sea of confusion, pain and brokenness. Thousands and thousands and thousands of men, women, and children who need a Savior. Thousands and thousands and thousands of men, women, and children who need what the church has to offer. Thousands and thousands and thousands of men, women, and children, slowly losing heart, drifting out in numbness and emptiness.

Do you see them? I think you do.

There is a person in your life who has had many

negative things happen lately. He never really had much of a relationship with God and now he doesn't want one. He may admit that God exists but he doesn't like Him that much. "Why would God do this to me?" he questions. He needs an answer. Are you going to give it to him?

There is a person in your world or at least close to it. She stands a little to the side. A neighbor that seldom comes out of her house. A coworker who doesn't join in with the group. Someone you know that never really seems to have much to say. A lonely person. She needs a place to belong. What are you going to do about it?

There is a couple you know fairly well. You know that their marriage is not good. How long it will last is anyone's guess. They need help. Will you be the one to give it to them?

You see people in the workforce who believe their self-worth is dependent on their net worth. They are driven and they like to drive others. Insecurity is masked with fast-talking. Weakness is pumped up with bravado. Getting ahead means putting others behind. Doubt is stifled with slogans and vision statements. Bankruptcy in terms of relationships is disguised with money and the things money can buy. But the façade is slowly crumbling. They need something solid—a "life ring" they can hang onto. Will you be the one to throw it?

You've seen this person. You know this person. He used to go to church. Everything seemed okay. But someone said something—you don't even know what it was. Someone did something or neglected to do something. The result: He no longer wants anything to do with church. What happened? What can be done about it? He needs to get reconnected. Will you be the one who helps make that happen?

You see your neighbors on a regular basis. Good people, really. Pleasant. Polite. When they drive by, they wave. They have a couple of kids and a dog. He works downtown; she has a part-time job closer to home. Their two kids go to the local school. At the end of the day the whole family watches TV. Saturday, the kids have soccer and piano lessons. Sunday, there are a few chores to do and then off to the park. Neither mom nor dad particularly like their jobs, but the money is needed. The kids don't particularly like school but that is just the way life goes. These neighbors of yours are just a typical, average family in North America. So what is wrong with this picture?

It's all they have. TV, soccer, work, school…There is no greater purpose that all of life fits into. When it comes to morality for the kids, well, whatever everyone else is doing will be the way it goes. Life is just something to get through, filling it with whatever you need to do to get through it.

What this family needs is to know that they have been created in the image of a loving, creative, purposeful God who is trying to make big things happen in this universe, and that He chooses to use people—families like theirs—to fulfill His purpose. Are you going to tell them this?

There is another person in the water. You don't like to think about it—it hurts. There is nothing in your life that hurts more. You have a family member or a close friend out in the water. How she got there is not important. You've tried to get her back into the lifeboat. You've thrown life rings. You've enlisted the help of others to rescue her. You've tried to force things. You've tried to just let things be. You've prayed until your knees were rubbed raw. But your spouse, your child, your friend—whoever it is—is still in the water and his or her silent scream for help burns a hole right through your heart. What can be done about this?

Yes, you hear the cries of those dying without Christ in their lives. You see them thrashing about trying to stay afloat. You know them. You know their names.

Take five minutes and write down their names:

_____	_____
_____	_____
_____	_____
_____	_____
_____	_____
_____	_____
_____	_____
_____	_____

How many names could you write down? If you could not think of very many, guess what? You are sitting too far to the center of the lifeboat. Get close to the edge so you can see the thousands thrashing in the waters around your boat.

If you had no trouble writing down some names, look at them. These names represent real people—made in the image of God—who are currently in the water. If they are not soon rescued, they will die—eternally. This is big. It is the biggest!

There is nothing more important on your agenda in life than these people. Their eternity hangs in the balance. You have no greater cause in life. God has chosen you as a recipient of His life-saving grace, and He calls you to pass it on to those nearby. The seat next to you in the lifeboat is open. Why aren't you filling it?

———————

Today's paper had a follow-up story on Timothy O'Brian. He killed himself thinking he had missed a huge jackpot—four million dollars. But coroner Roy Barter said O'Brian misread the numbers drawn. If he had bought a lottery ticket with the numbers he and his friend always chose they would have won only $59.

Timothy O'Brian threw his life away for missing out on...$29.50—his half of the winnings.

How many Timothy O'Brian's are out there—lost, confused, looking for something solid to hold on to—to live for?

Speaking in Liverpool, Coroner Roy Barter suggested that lottery jackpots should be smaller to ease the pressure of what "could potentially become a serious social problem." No kidding! But the lottery is not the social problem. It is just one really poor solution to the social problem, or perhaps, spiritual problem that is already serious—millions who need a Savior—millions who need a way out, or maybe just a way.

"I am the way, the truth and the life," Jesus told his followers. People need a Savior. The church has been sent out by Christ Himself to show cold, shivering, dying people the way.

So, in the light of the obvious need, why are churches half empty?

In the face of the list of names you just made, why is there an empty seat next to you in church?

Questions:

1. What got your attention in this chapter and what might God be trying to say to you through it?
2. Can you share with the group some of the names you wrote down in this chapter?
3. Why is it sometimes hard to make the people represented by the names you wrote down a top priority in terms of your prayer life, your time, and your energy?

CHAPTER THREE
People Are Afraid

Then Agrippa said to Paul, "Do you think that in such a short time you can persuade me to be a Christian?"

Act 26:28

The tickets were $100 each. I wanted to go but I'd have to take my wife—$200 for the two of us. No matter how good the band was or how much nostalgia I would get out of it, that was just too much for a concert. But when the event was finished, I wished we had gone. Maybe $200 to take a nostalgic trip back to formative days of my youth would be worth it. Too late. I guess I'll just have to "Get Over It." In case you are not a fan of the Eagles—popular in the '70s and popular again in 1995 with a tour and new hit song "Get Over It"—it was their concert I had missed.

Friends of mine, who did not have as many misgivings about spending that kind of money on a concert (or perhaps they just have more money), said it was great—mostly the old songs, and a few new ones.

I take consolation in the knowledge that I have the CD—only $14.95. What a deal!

There are many great songs on this album, some new, some old. The last song is my favorite—an oldie. It describes our society. It describes the people in your city and mine—thousands of men, women, and children all alone—needing a Savior. The song ends with the line: "You better let somebody love you before it's too late." Good description of lost people so cold and numb they resist being rescued. The song is called: "Desperado."

I built a lifeboat for desperadoes a few years ago. I rented one anyway—a big one—the size of a gym. Actually, it was a gym. That was the setting for my church that did not yet exist. The question then was: "How does one fill it?"

I thought it would be easier than it turned out to be.

It should have been easy, right? I mean thousands of men, women, and children are gasping for air, grasping for anything that floats. How hard could it be to pick up a few?

I thought I'd test the waters. With clipboard in hand I headed out to my neighborhood with a couple of questions.

> **Steve:** Hi, my name is Steve Elzinga and I am a new Pastor in the area looking to start a new church. I want to meet the needs of my new community so I was wondering if I could ask you a couple questions. (That was my opening line when someone answered the doorbell.)
>
> **Neighbor:** O...kay. (This was often said with much hesitation.)
>
> **Steve:** Do you go to church?
>
> Neighbor: No.
>
> **Steve:** No? Great! (Perfect! A person drowning in the great sea of despair.)
>
> **Steve:** Why do you think most people don't go to church?
>
> **Neighbor:** Well, it's boring. The whole thing is like out of the dark ages. Messages are so deep I don't think most ministers even know what they're talking about. What does it have to do with everyday life?
>
> **Steve:** "O...kay. If you were thinking of going to church, not that you are, but if you were thinking about going to church, what would you want to see there?
>
> **Neighbor:** If you don't have a sermon, I'll come to your church.
>
> **Steve:** Oh, okay. That is interesting.

I remember walking away thinking: Who does this guy think he is? I went to college for four years. Then I went to seminary for four more years. I gave up opportunities to make money. I have dedicated my life to helping stranded people find safety in the lifeboat of the church and this guy doesn't want it.

Here I was, out of my comfort zone, trying to help someone in the water. He is going down. I have an empty seat right next to me in my lifeboat (I had 300 empty seats in my lifeboat). I have my hand stretched out to him. He acts like I am trying to get him to buy a vacuum cleaner or something. I am offering life and he is not sure he can be bothered with it.

Here is the heart of the problem. The seat next to me is empty. The seat next to you is empty. And even if these seats are occupied we could always squeeze in a few more people. I want to offer a lifeboat seat to someone. I don't know of any church that doesn't want people to come in and be saved. I don't know of any Christian that doesn't want the new life in Christ for a neighbor, a friend, or a coworker. It's just that many of those we think need saving don't want to be saved. They don't want to come to church. They don't want to have what we have. What are we supposed to do?

———————

Our next-door neighbors sold their house to some out-of-towners. Before they moved in someone had tipped them off. Who? I don't know. How was it done? I don't know. I suspect there is some secret organization out there alerting home buyers when they move in next to a minister. Somehow our new neighbors knew. And I don't think they were thrilled with it.

I am not exactly sure what the big deal is living next to a minister. But it seems that many people are worried more about what a minister may think of them than what God thinks of them. Most people know that God is everywhere and He sees and knows all. Most people don't let this fact change their lives. If a person is not concerned about how God sees their life, why would they worry about how a minister sees it? Maybe it is because they cannot see God—out of sight, out of mind—but they can see the minister, possibly every day.

Anyway, the day our new neighbors moved in, my wife took the opportunity to welcome them to the neighborhood. Our new neighbor leaned over the fence and said, "I'll talk. I love to talk, but not about religion. Don't try to get us to come to your church." As I said, someone had tipped them off. Now what were we supposed to do? They were drowning right next to our home. We were standing at the fence with a life ring in hand. But the very ones going down did not want the life ring. They didn't even want to talk about the life ring.

Most of us have, at some point in our lives, asked someone, somewhere, somehow, to go to church with us. We all realize that we have been saved through no merit of our own and want to share that salvation with those who might need it. But the people we have asked, often it seems, are not that eager to be saved. Why? Let me give you a few reasons why people resist assistance.

(Oh, by the way, our neighbors who refused to talk about Christianity with us eventually became members of our church—in God's timing.)

First, there are those who resist being saved because they believe they don't need it. He should have known better. At least that is how we see things so many years after the fact. As it was he got six warnings of a potentially dangerous situation. After each warning he did nothing.

But why should he? He was the most seasoned, most respected, most popular, most experienced captain in the most prominent ocean liner company in the world. And when the White Star Line wanted a captain to take their newest, largest, most expensive ship out on her maiden voyage, he was their man—Captain Edward J. Smith. He was the obvious choice. This voyage was to be the pinnacle of a career that lasted over 40 years.

He had successfully commanded no fewer than 17 different White Star vessels. He was bold; he was confident. As commander of the *Adriatic* in 1906 he was quoted as saying, "I cannot imagine any condition which would cause a ship to founder. I cannot conceive of any vital disaster happening to this vessel. Modern ship building has gone beyond that."

In 1911 he had successfully taken the *Titanic*'s sister ship, the *Olympic*, on its maiden voyage. So on April 14, 1912, as Captain Smith stood on the bridge of the *Titanic*, the cold bitter wind in his face, it was all engines full ahead—never mind warnings of ice.

He should have known better. But he didn't. Neither do we.

We know intellectually that we will die. Everyone dies. We know it, but we don't believe it. How does one picture oneself as not being around, as not existing, as being no more? All our lives we have experienced being alive. How then are we to think about what is impossible to experience, namely, death? As long as we are alive we cannot know what death is like and when we finally do die, we are at that moment robbed of our experience of it.

People should know better, but many do not. People should know that you can only tread water in this life for 70 years or so, and then you go down. As human beings, we are not "unsinkable." Unless somebody saves you, you will sink into the depths of decay.

The people you want to reach out to with the life-saving gospel of Jesus Christ should know better, but denial is a powerful thing. We live in a culture that spends a lot of time and energy denying the inevitable. Graying hair is dyed. Telling wrinkles are treated with Botox. Yogurt and exercise are the springs of living water. Staying busy with shopping, sports, weekend outings, and work is the strategy of choice for many in their quest to forget about death.

Second, there are those who resist being saved because they don't want to leave the party. We had five days in Hawaii back in '81. My wife and I were en route to the Philippines for a year of missionary work. The stopover in Honolulu was no extra charge. Being of Dutch stock (a few generations back), we took advantage of this opportunity. We found accommodations for $20 a day and tried to make the most of it. We won a couple of tickets for a sunset dinner cruise aboard a large Catamaran.

On board we heard someone say, "Welcome to the Party Boat!" We soon learned why. The Mai Tais were free and everyone on board took advantage of it. By the time we reached port, everyone was feeling no pain.

That is the attraction of a good party. To get away from the pain. To forget the drudgery of life. To escape the unanswered questions.

"Let's eat and drink and be merry for tomorrow we die." Paul wrote these words 2,000 years ago. He was writing to people who were questioning the resurrection of Jesus Christ from the dead—questioning the resurrection of anyone. These folks believed that when you get to the end of life's road, all you'll find is a dead end—a depressing way to look at life because you're left with only two options: be depressed or party!

Many choose to party. Some party with booze. Some party with drugs. Some party with sports. Some party with food. Some party by making money. Some party by spending it. Some party by watching movies—whatever it takes to forget you are depressed.

But here is the rub. If you choose the party you won't want to leave it. Because if you leave the party, you will have to face reality or at least the question of what reality is. That is too sobering for most party lovers. Better to stay drunk with denial.

When you try to reach out to a person that is in denial about their mortality, they may resist you. From your point-of-view you are only trying to bring the possibility of some hope to their empty, wasted lives. But from their point-of-view you are trying to drag them from the only thing they have in life—the party.

The *Titanic* was the Party Boat of the early 1900s. Sir Philip Gibbs, a journalist in 1912, wrote: *"All that the genius of modern life has invented for comfort and adorn-*

ment was lavished upon her...all that wealth and art can attain in splendor was given to her decoration...The richest man on earth would not lack a single comfort that his wealth might buy."

First class passengers enjoyed the finest rooms, food, and service ever seen afloat. The heated swimming pool, the gymnasium, the squash court, and the grand ballroom were just a few of the ship's uncommon pleasures. Almost half the people on board the *Titanic* were members of the crew. They were all hired to pamper, cater, coddle, and indulge the passengers—especially those sailing first class. If you only go around once in life, and you don't want to face the fact that you only go around once in life, then first class is the way to go, isn't it?

Many of the *Titanic's* lifeboats left the sinking ship half empty because many of the first class passengers couldn't pull themselves from the party—the luxury. They didn't want to be bothered. It was cold outside. The thought of leaving was too painful. Besides, who knew if the ship was really going down? They didn't want to get into a lifeboat for nothing. They, in their denial, went down with the ship.

Third, there are those who resist being saved because they are not willing to leave the security of the sinking ship. I've always wanted to go on a cruise. Exotic destinations attract me. Paying once and pretending everything is free is another attraction. Cruise ships dock not 18 miles from the house our family lived in when we were planting a church just outside of Vancouver. You can say many things about cruise ships, but in my mind there is just one word needed: BIG!

The *Titanic* was big even by today's standards. She measured 882 feet long. Picture an 88-story building on its side. From the water line to the deck was 75 feet. She weighed 46,000 tons. A single link of the ship's anchor chain weighed 175 pounds, and 20  horses were needed just to haul each of her three anchors to the shipyard. Her design was praised as a marvel of engineering. *The Shipbuilder* magazine labeled her "practically unsinkable."

It took three years to build, but after only four days in active service, out in the middle of the Atlantic Ocean, just before midnight, the *Titanic* hit an iceberg and was mortally wounded. In the first-class smoking room, some men were playing cards. They detected a slight jolt, but they ignored it and went on with their card game. Closer to the front of the ship, one of the firemen was awakened by the collision. Climbing out of bed, he went out to look on the deck and saw that it was covered with small pieces of broken ice. "Oh, we have struck an iceberg," he said to himself. "That is nothing." Then he returned to his bunk and went back to sleep. Captain Smith ordered that the engines be shut down, halting the ship's motion through the water. The steady hum the passengers became accustomed to over the previous four days was silenced. Their curiosity was awakened.

Throughout the ship, people began investigating. In first class, passengers crawled out of their warm beds, put bathrobes over their pajamas, and wandered out into the hallway to ask the stewards what the problem was. The stewards didn't know. "There is no cause for alarm," one said.

Rumors began to circulate. "We've hit a whale." "A propeller has been broken and we have to go back to Belfast for repairs." (Six months earlier, *Titanic*'s sister ship lost a propeller.)

Soon people realized that the ship at least came close to an iceberg. A huge chunk of ice had fallen onto the starboard deck and was attracting a crowd. Still, the ice caused no alarm, but was regarded as a curiosity. People danced around the ice and joked about putting pieces of it in their drinks. One of the ship's workers broke off a chunk and slipped it under the covers of a mate who was still in bed.

Captain Smith was not taking the situation lightly. He sent for Thomas Andrews, the designer of the *Titanic*. When Andrews arrived on the bridge, the two men made a quick tour of the bow of the ship to see the damage for themselves. They soon learned the worst.

On E Deck, they found that the squash court was filling up rapidly; water was now up to the foul line. Crew members reported that the mail room on F Deck was completely flooded, and bags of mail were floating up to the next deck. Seawater was squirting into boiler rooms No. 5 and 6. Adding it all up, Captain Smith and Andrews figured there had to be a 300-foot tear along the starboard hull. The unsinkable was sinking fast.

By midnight, 20 minutes after the collision, Captain Smith gave the order to get the lifeboats ready.

It took Captain Smith only a few minutes to figure out that the greatest ship on earth could not save anyone—only the 20 lifeboats could. It took the passengers of the *Titanic* a little longer to figure it out.

Imagine you were on the *Titanic* that cold, winter night. You are on the largest moving object in the world, the maiden voyage of the most sophisticated ship ever built. You are tired. Poorly dressed. The temperature is below freezing. You are somewhere—who knows where—in the middle of the ocean. It is pitch black out there and crew members want you to get into a tiny, wooden boat that is precariously hanging 70 feet over the side of the ship.

It was so cold outside that many preferred to stay in the lounges and smoking rooms where it was warm and where it still seemed like a safe place to be. John Jacob Astor, the richest man on board and one of the richest men in the world, is quoted as saying, "We are safer here than in that little boat."

Who in their right mind would leave the security of a 900-foot ship for a 30-foot boat?

That's how many people view church from the outside. When you ask someone to go to your church, it's like asking them to step off from the security of their world—sinking though it may be—and into a scary little boat that is adrift in a black, cold sea, on a dark night. The familiar, as bad as it might be, sometimes feels more secure.

Observe where new visitors to your church sit. In my church they sit close to the door. Why? They feel very insecure, and if things get too scary they want to be close enough to the door for a quick exit. And why shouldn't they feel that way? They don't know God. They don't know His love. They are not too sure about you either. They have no idea that your church is a place where they will be treated with love and dignity. They are often extremely doubtful that your church is a place where they can belong.

Fourth, there are those who resist being saved because they are too numb to care. Originally from Michigan and having spent many of my summers swimming and boating in the warm lakes there, I never really understood how a person could die while floating about in the water. But after living only 10 miles from the Pacific Ocean for a period of nine years, I get it. Ocean water can be cold. I mean really cold! So cold I bought myself a dry-suit. Even then, I'm cold within 30 minutes.

There are many people that are just too numb to care about change—good or bad. Many do not like their situation but they like change less. They would rather have the problem they know than the possibility they do not.

Her name is…well, it doesn't really matter. You know her or someone like her. She was that one person in your class that didn't fit in very well. Do you want to know how she felt about being left out? Here is a letter from the person I knew.

Do you know what it is like to live without love? Do you know what it is like going to your fourth grade class every day listening to other kids fight over who has to sit next to you—like your proximity was some kind of penalty? My

41

fellow classmates would tease me about my clothes. I tried to explain to my hopelessly out-of-date parents what other kids were wearing but they were already 60 years old and couldn't understand, or wouldn't understand. At recess, best friends would go off and play and talk and laugh and live. I was left alone. What could I do? I tried to be a part of things—from a distance. I would casually get close to some of my classmates so I could see them or maybe just hear them and pretend that I belonged. Sometimes I would get too close and they would call me a hurtful name and run away.

The worst thing that they did, or did not do... they did not touch me. No one took my hand and said, "Come on, let's play." No one held me when I was sad or afraid. No one hugged me just to say, "You're my friend." I was untouchable. When you are only 10 years old and the people in your life freak out like they caught some horrible contagious disease because they accidentally brushed against your skin, you begin to wonder what kind of evil creature you really are. When I bathed, I used to scrub my skin pink trying to rub off whatever offended everyone. When I prayed, I pleaded with God to create something new. But there was no escape. There was nothing I could do.

I think I understand now. It is as if everyone thinks that someone has to be last, someone has to be ugly, someone has to be on the bottom, someone has to be stupid, someone has to be left out, someone has to be blamed, someone has to suffer and if I was that someone, then they were safe. And everyone's fear is that if they get too close, if they dare to love the unlovable, touch the untouchable, save the lost, they too might be crucified.

I didn't understand when I was 10. Instead, I learned to cope—to live without love. But sometimes, in a weak moment, when a courageous person risked their own self-worth and was nice to me, I found myself hoping. For what? A friend. A friend who didn't care what I wore or what I looked like. A friend who was glad to see me and wanted to know what I was thinking and feeling inside. A friend to eat lunch with, to walk down the sidewalk with after school. All I ever wanted was a friend.

But hoping for a friend that never comes is harder than having no hope at all. So I usually ended up pushing away would-be friends. I learned to cope, to live without love.

There are many people too cold and too numb to hope for a loving, caring hand reaching down to rescue them from the paralyzing chill of loneliness.

Fifth, there are those who resist being saved because they assume they are in the lifeboat already. It happened at about the fourth hole. That's when it typically happens. The first three holes of golf, when playing with people you've never met before, are taken up with the exchange of names and golf handicaps. By the fourth hole someone gets around to asking what the others do for a living.

> "I'm a banker."
> "Oh really."
> "I'm in construction."
> "Oh, interesting."
> "I'm a Pastor."
> "Oh..."

At this point, everyone tries to recall what kind of language they used on the second hole when their tee shot went into the woods.

That is how the conversation usually goes. This time it was different. Ernie, when he found out I was a pastor, responded rather confidently, "I am a Catholic myself but I don't go to church. I don't think a person has to go to church to get to Heaven. Besides, God is more real to me out here in the trees and grass."

I decided to press his confidence a little: "What makes you think you are going to Heaven?"

He proceeded to tell me about all the good stuff he did in life, like not treating his wife badly, giving to the Salvation Army at Christmas, and generally being an all-around good citizen. I asked him how he knew that this is what it took to get to Heaven. He wasn't sure but figured God was a loving God and any reasonable attempt at living a good life would be acceptable.

There are many Ernies in the world. They think they are in the lifeboat. Their lives are a mess, there is brokenness at every turn, but they still believe somehow that they are in the lifeboat.

Sixth, there are those who resist being saved because

they just don't know enough about lifeboats. I own a boat. A sailboat. Actually, I own two of them. Lasers. The kind used in the Olympics. With ownership comes a whole new language. *Starboard, sheets, port, tack, stern, aft, etc.* I have become comfortable in the sailboat world. I know what I am doing.

I enjoy taking non-sailors for a sail in the water and sun. They get aboard…with some fear. They look to me for guidance. They want to be of some value on the boat. They want to feel like they belong.

"Grab the sheet," I command. They think I'm talking about the sail. "The rope, the rope," I clarify.

"The rope?" they ask. "Why do you call it a sheet?"

"Because that's what the rope on a sailboat is called," I respond, not without some annoyance.

"I don't get that."

And so it goes. I understand and appreciate the sailing world. The newcomer doesn't really get it yet. It's confusing. It's complicated. It's stupid…to him.

When a person who's not that familiar with church ventures in, it often seems confusing. It seems complicated. It may even seem stupid.

We, in the church world, often without realizing it, have our own church language. *Justification, Lamb of God, Zion, sin, rapture, sanctification, etc.*

A newcomer understands that the Bible is a book. He doesn't understand when the pastor begins his sermon with, "Will you please turn with me to the book of John."

"What is the book of John?" they want to know. They observe others turning pages in their Bibles. They are amazed to learn that the book of John is a book in the larger book called the Bible. "Very strange," they say.

The songs that are sung in church often sound like

music from an era that they are not familiar with.

The sermon. They wonder why they can't really piece together what this person is talking about.

I could go on and on. You get the point. Or do you? Some of you are saying in the back of your mind that you don't believe I am being accurate about how newcomers feel. You may think I am exaggerating. Am I?

It is hard sometimes to really understand how people who aren't raised in our own culture can be so radically different than we are. Because something has always been true for us all of our lives, we have a hard time understanding how others can miss what we have always taken for granted.

If you think I am exaggerating, here is what I want you to do. Find someone who was not raised in the church and invite that person to your church. Ask them how it went. If they are honest, you will learn something. If you have never done this, perhaps you assume you know more about what non-churched people think than you actually do.

Seventh, there are those who resist being saved for reasons incomprehensible. He's telling me about his life. His father was abusive. The abuse stopped when his father ran off with some woman he met. His mother: an alcoholic. She died young. He never graduated from high school; went from job to job; in jail eight times—once for three years; three kids by three different women; drug abuse for over ten years; various recovery programs—15 in all. I asked him if he would like to try living life by the book—the good book—the Bible. He scratched his head and said, "I'm not sure I want to give up my freedom."

I can't tell you how many times I have had this conversation with someone I was trying to get into the lifeboat:

"Do you believe in God?"
"Yes."
"Do you know much about God?"
"No."
"Would you like help getting to know Him?"
"No."

Eighth, there are those who aren't necessarily resisting being saved, but have never been invited to get in a lifeboat. A nationwide study done by Barna Research found that one out of four people who don't currently go to church would willingly attend a church service if a friend invited them to do so. Do you believe this study?

Let's do a bit of dreaming. If we can believe the results of this study, what would happen if every family in your church were to invite four non-churchgoing families to your church this week? Your church would double in attendance in one week. How simple can church growth get?

So why won't you try this? Two reasons.

One, you fear rejection. If you have to invite four friends in order to get one "yes," that means three people you know will, in one way or another, reject your invitation. That is a 75 percent failure rate. The fear of rejection—the fear of failure—keeps many of us from reaching our hand out of the boat.

Two, you just don't believe that there are people not going to church who really, truly want to go. Why? It's not because we checked it out. It's just that it doesn't make any sense to us that someone who wants to go to church wouldn't just go.

The truth is, you can randomly call 100 people you

have never met and invite them to your church, and ten will say yes. And of the ten that have said yes, one will actually come. I know this is true because that is how I started my church in Surrey. We made 20,000 phone calls over a two-week period. Out of the 20,000 people we called, 2,000 said they wanted more information regarding our grand opening. Finally, out of the 2,000 that seemed interested, 200 came to our opening service.

People are not as resistant as we think. Thousands upon thousands of men, women, and children in the water are looking for a hand to pull them up.

If that is true, why aren't we pulling them in?

Questions:
1. What got your attention in this chapter and what might God be trying to say to you through it?
2. In this chapter we looked at the reasons people have for not getting into the lifeboat called the church. Before you became a Christian or got serious about your faith, which of the reasons stated would you have related to?
3. How do the people on your list (from the previous chapter) match up to some of the reasons talked about in this chapter?
4. Can you think of other reasons people might have for not wanting to get "saved" by the lifeboat called the church?

CHAPTER FOUR
We Are Saved (High and Dry)

"God bless…

me, my wife…

my brother Jake and his wife…

us four, no more…

Amen!"

Lifeboat No. 8, the second port-side lifeboat to be lowered, contained 24 women and four crew members. It could have held Mrs. Isidor Straus, wife of the founder of Macy's department store, but she chose to stay with her husband. Second Officer Lightoller loaded it with all the women and children he could see but there were still many empty seats. The women on board begged Captain Smith to let some of the husbands come into the lifeboat to row, but "women and children only" was the order.

Officer Lightoller put Seaman Jones in command and instructed him to row for the light that could be seen in the distance. Jones put the Countess of Rothes in charge of the tiller, commenting, "She had a lot to say so I put her to steering the boat." They rowed toward the light they assumed was a ship but it never seemed to get any closer. Mrs. J. Stuart White testified at the American Investigation that, "The women in our boat all rowed... the men did not know the first thing about it."

After the *Titanic* sank, Seaman Jones proposed that they row back and try to rescue some of the people struggling in the water. But he was greeted with a wail of protest from most of the very women who earlier had pleaded for their husband's lives.

Lifeboat No. 8—28 people in a boat designed to hold 65—did not row back.

Third Officer Herbert Pitman was at the tiller of Lifeboat No. 5. When the *Titanic* finally went under, he instinctively turned his boat around shouting "Now, men, we will pull toward the wreck!" What else should they do? Lifeboats save people. The cries of desperate men, women, and children came from only a few hundred yards away. But never underestimate the power of fear.

One of the ladies in the boat begged the men not to

row back. "Why should we lose our lives in a useless attempt to save others?"

The fear spread. Others joined the protest. Pitman wavered in his resolve and for the next hour, as the cries of 1,500 people became fainter, Lifeboat No. 5 rowed slowly, silently away. Forty people in a boat designed to hold 65.

In Lifeboat No. 2, Fourth Officer Boxhall asked, "Shall we go back?" With the cries of hundreds of people only yards away ringing in their ears, the saved ones in Lifeboat No. 2 unanimously said, "No."

Lifeboat No. 2—25 in a boat designed to hold 40—did not go back.

Things were different in Lifeboat No. 6. One of the ladies on board was Mrs. Lucian Smith. In the final moments that Mrs. Smith had with her husband on the deck of the *Titanic*, he said to her, "I never expected to ask you to obey, but this is one time you must. It is only a matter of form to have women and children first. The ship is thoroughly equipped and everyone on her will be saved."

As he said these words to his distraught wife he must have known that they would never be together again. Mrs. Smith asked him if he was being completely truthful. Mr. Smith gave a firm, deceptive, "Yes." They kissed each other good-bye and as the lifeboat dropped to the sea, he called from the deck, "Keep your hands in your pockets; it is very cold weather."

Now, having watched the ship go down and realizing that one of the cries for help must be from her husband who had tricked her into getting into the lifeboat, Mrs. Smith begged Quartermaster Hitchens to row back. Other women in the boat wanted to go back as well.

But Hitchens refused. He warned them of the dangers in going back. People, half-crazed in panic would most surely swamp or even capsize the boat and all would be lost. What could the women say? Hitchens was the seaman. They trusted him to know what he was talking about. Lifeboat No. 6—capacity 65; occupants 28—did not row back.

Did you catch that? Only 28 in the boat. That means there were 37 empty seats. Thirty-seven people could have been saved if they had only rowed back.

In boat after boat the story was the same. A call to go back. A strong negative reaction. Another lifeboat slowly rowing away. Men, women, and children—just yards away—drowning.

In church after church, sadly, the story is the same. There is a call to go back. This is greeted with a strong negative reaction. The result? Another church slowly rowing away. Men, women, and children—thousands, no millions of them—just yards away, drowning, eternally.

Boat 1 - 40 1.10	Boat 2 – 40 – 1.45	Boat 3 – 65 – 1.00	Boat 4 – 65 – 1.55	Boat 5 – 65 – 12.55
5 First Class	8 First Class	25 First Class	23 First Class	31 First Class
7 Crew	10 Thrid Class	15 Crew	1 Servant	7 Crew
	3 Crew	1 dog	6 Third Class	
	4 others		12 Crew	
Boat 6 – 65 – 12.55	**Boat 7 – 65 – 12.45**	**Boat 8 – 65 – 1.10**	**Boat 9 – 65 – 1.20**	Boat 10 – 65 – 1.20
20 First Class	22 First Class	26 First Class	**6 First Class**	9 First Class
2 Crew	3 Crew	4 Crew	**17 Second Class**	17 Second Class
6 Others	3 Others	2 Others	**3 Third Class**	6 Third Class
1 dog	1 dog		**15 Crew**	4 Crew
Boat 11 – 65 – 1.25	**Boat 12 – 65 – 1.25**	**Boat 13 – 65 – 1.35**	**Boat 14 – 65 – 1.30**	**Boat 15 – 65 – 1.35**
5 First Class	15 Second Class	1 First Class	4 First Class	1 First Class
14 Second Class	1 Third Class	13 Second Class	24 Second Class	1 Second Class
6 Third Class	4 Crew	27 Third Class	4 Third Class	38 Third Class
24 Crew		24 Crew	15 Crew	25 Crew
Boat 16 – 65 – 1.35	**Collapsible A – 47**	**Collapsible B – 47**	**Collapsible C – 47**	**Collapsible D – 47**
3 Second Class	3 First Class	3 First Class	**– 1.40**	**– 2.05**
23 Third Class	8 Third Class	1 Second Class	2 First Class	7 First Class
11 Crew	5 Crew	5 Third Class	36 Third Class	2 Second Class
		18 Crew	6 Crew	9 Third Class
				7 Crew

Why? In the face of the obvious need, why didn't the lifeboats go back?

Why? In the face of the obvious need, why don't churches go back?

Some reasons:

If we go after the lost what will happen to our church, our traditions?

If we grow as a church we will lose the close family feeling that we enjoy so much.

We will weaken our boat if we start scooping people out of the water. Translation: We will probably water down the gospel to get people to come to our church.

If we are successful in getting lost people in our church, what influence will their children have on my children? God forbid, one of my kids starts dating one of these water-soaked newcomers.

New people won't appreciate our traditions and values.

All the energy of the leadership will get soaked up by these new, needy people. What about us, the faithful?

I might get wet.

We may lose everything we have worked so hard to get.

If people want to be saved, they know where our boat is. The doors are always open. Let them swim to us.

We've got to make sure that the people we have in our boats already are safe and warm before we go back and get any more.

Sound familiar? These are the same excuses the passengers in lifeboats—in 1912 in the middle of the Atlantic Ocean—used for not going back. No doubt you've used some of these, too. I know I have.

We have something; we fear losing it.

We have the truth; we fear losing it, or at least we fear that in our zeal to reach others, the truth will be watered down.

When one is involved in the rescue business there is always the threat of getting watered down. *Titanic* lifeboats were afraid of getting sucked under when the Goliath ship went down. Lifeboat passengers rowed hard to get away. After the ship sank, they did not row back for fear of getting watered down with desperate, drowning people.

Their fear was legitimate. What good is a lifeboat if its integrity—its ability to be a lifeboat—is compromised because it fills up with water?

But what good is a dry lifeboat with a solid crew that does very little rescuing of drowning people?

The truth is, lifeboats should attempt rescues despite the fear of being watered down. That is the job of a lifeboat. One has to trust the integrity of the lifeboat, the lifeboat maker and those rowing the lifeboat.

Trust seems to be lacking these days. It is almost assumed by some church leaders that if your church is reaching lost people and growing you must be compromising the gospel and accommodating the world. It is assumed you are compromising the integrity of your lifeboat.

In my opinion, church leaders that only talk about holding onto the truth but never or seldom actually risk being a lifeboat should be very careful when they question the integrity of lifeboat churches that actually take the risk of getting watered down as they actually do the work of the lifeboats. Or to say it bluntly: If you are not actually risking a rescue attempt of a non-churched person yourself, perhaps you are not in position to criticize those who are.

Lifeboats that do not row back are not lifeboats—they are pleasure crafts. And I believe that lifeboat churches that actually do lifeboat church work, far from letting go of the truth, understand and hold on to it all the more. Why? Because every day is a matter of life or death. There is immediate feedback with a lifeboat that is committed to rescue work. If you compromise the truth, you may get a drowning person in your boat, but you then watch them die anyway. In the end you die, too. If the lifeboat gets watered down, all in the lifeboat perish.

So, why is there this fear of losing the truth? Maybe we, people in lifeboats, who are not currently involved in lifeboat work, deep down, fear we ourselves have lost the truth.

We have our traditions; we fear losing them.

Traditions are cultural carriers of truth. As human beings we need traditions that we can hang everyday living on. The Bible, for example, will do us very little good unless we develop patterns of accessing it and applying it to our lives. These patterns, adopted and reinforced by a group of people, become traditions. Many churchgoers follow, for example, a Sunday morning tradition of accessing the Bible through a learned person who explains it in a lecture fashion. Many of us have a tradition of reading the Bible at the dinner table with our families. These traditions guide and direct us as we try to understand and apply God's word to our lives. These and a myriad more just like them have been developed over many years by groups of people united around these traditions.

New people to the group are often a threat to these history-laden traditions. New folks will not hold them as dear as the old folks. Traditions are adopted slowly. Newcomers have a tendency to change traditions quickly—always for the worse in the eyes of the old-timers.

So churches hold on to their traditions and are fearful and resistant to new folks coming on board. But many of these same churches are also fearful of stagnation, decline, and the loss of their youth. This fear of decline in numbers makes churches more interested in outreach. But if a church is successful in outreach, it stands a good chance of losing its traditions.

My own denomination seems to be caught in this sinking whirlpool. On the one hand, many churches in my denomination, because of declining numbers and the loss of youth, are taking a serious look at outreach. On the other hand, church leaders and seminary professors are waving the "we are going to lose our traditions" flag because churches are exploring ways to engage in outreach.

My thought is this: if your tradition is keeping you from rowing back in an attempt to rescue people dying without Christ, then perhaps the possibility of losing one's traditions, or at least the part that is keeping your from rowing back, is worth considering. A church that is not engaged in outreach, that is not pulling people out of the water, is, in my opinion, all wet.

We have power and position; we fear losing them.

In ninth grade I played shortstop on our school softball team. We had nine players on the team. No one ever sat on the bench. At the year's end we joined a summer league. We had 10 players that summer. Our tenth player only got to play if one of the other nine couldn't make it. The original nine never sat on the bench. That is the way we wanted it. Others wanted to join our team but we told them to start their own team.

That is the way I wanted it. Shortstop was my position. I played shortstop every inning of every game we played that year. I did not want to share it with anyone else. It didn't matter if someone else was a better short-stop. Shortstop was my position—for five glorious years. Then the team folded.

I loved playing shortstop. I loved playing with my friends. We were close. We accepted each other for what each one was. We forgave each other for the errors and the strikeouts and we cheered each other for the hits and the great plays. We were a team. We were a great team. We were a winning team. We had the trophies to prove it.

We had something; we didn't want to share it with anyone else for fear that we would lose "the winning team."

I had something; I didn't want to share it with anyone else for fear that I would lose my "position" on that winning team.

Perhaps your church feels like a great winning team. Each one knows the other. The positions were handed out a long time ago. You don't mind a few new folks joining but let me ask you: Where do most of the new folks end up? On the field, on the bench, or worse yet, in the stands?

In '88 my wife and I planted a new church with nine other Christian families. We were a great team. We did outreach. Hundreds came from the community. After two years I did a study on the leadership positions in our successful outreach church. I discovered that there wasn't a single original team member that had success-fully passed along a leadership position to any of the new players. The only new players that we had in positions of leadership were in those positions because new players created their own programs. When I presented my study to the original players they insisted that most new players just preferred to sit on the bench.

We have faith; we fear losing it.

He was asking me why I believed the Bible was the Word of God. I knew this one. I had memorized the necessary proof texts while in seminary.

I rattled off 2 Timothy 3:16,17: *All Scripture is God-breathed and is useful for teaching, rebuking, correcting and training in righteousness, so that the man of God may be thoroughly equipped for every good work.*

He seemed unimpressed, so I proceeded with 2 Peter 1:21: *For prophecy never had its origin in the will of man, but men spoke from God as they were carried along by the Holy Spirit.*

When my professor used these verses in class we were sold. But when I recited them for my unbelieving friend, he was not buying. I explained these verses and even threw in a bit of church history. Somehow the words I said did not sound as convincing in my own ears as they used to.

You want to give your faith a test? Go talk to someone that doesn't share your faith.

We have faith; we fear losing it. Or perhaps we fear we may not have had it in the first place.

We have many things; we fear losing them. We fear losing the truth. We fear losing our traditions. We fear losing our power and position. We, perhaps, fear losing even our faith. This is a lot of fear.

So...

Protect.
Defend.
Build walls.
Avoid the enemy.

The "Fortress" mentality

I grew up in a Christian fortress. My parents were Christians. My grandparents on both sides were Christians. So were my uncles and aunts and cousins, not to mention the neighbors, the barber, the baker, and the candlestick maker.

I was mentored in the "fortress" mentality in my home, church, and school. I learned a lot of good stuff in the fortress. But most of the good stuff I learned was only useful inside the fortress and most of it was about making the walls strong. I learned very little about how to operate outside the walls and help those outside the walls become strong.

Security was within the walls. Fear was outside. I grew up in a Christian community that lived in fear that darkness was stronger than light, that people on the outside were more likely to have an affect on people on the inside, that the person drowning in the water was more likely to pull the person in the lifeboat overboard than the person in the lifeboat was to pull the person in the water to the safety.

Because of our fear of what we might lose, we often isolated ourselves from those to whom we might lose it. All the while we told ourselves that the isolation was there to make us strong so that one day we would march out through the gate of our fortress to save the world.

But why would a person who is brought up in the fortress ever march out into the world? If, for example, a parent goes to great lengths to convince a child that the world is a scary place outside the wall, by the time the child has grown up, why wouldn't the child believe this to be true? And if a child grows up watching every adult he knows spend most of their effort and time working inside the fortress, when he grows up, why wouldn't he spend his effort and time working inside the fortress as well?

We fear that if we share what we have, we might lose it.

I pray that you may be active in sharing your faith, so that you will have a full understanding of every good thing we have in Christ.

Philemon 1:6

Could it be that lifeboats that risk rescuing people become stronger lifeboats? I believe the lifeboat church is stronger than most church members realize. It actually takes a lot to sink one.

All the lifeboats on the *Titanic* were not fully deployed when the ship went down. There were two makeshift lifeboats on top of the officer's quarters. In the dying moment of the *Titanic*, a crowd of men struggled to deploy two collapsible lifeboats, known as Collapsible Boats A and B. Collapsible Boat A eventually floated off and became half swamped with water. Collapsible Boat B was pushed to the edge of the roof and slid down on a couple of oars. It landed upside down. It doesn't get much worse for a lifeboat.

This upside-down lifeboat became the largest floating piece of debris within reach of 1,500 swimmers. Eventually, 30 men crawled up its half-submerged hull and stood balancing precariously on the badly compromised boat.

I have a picture of Collapsible Boat B taken a week after the disaster by crewmen from a ship sent to recovery the bodies and salvage what they could. In the picture, Collapsible Boat B is upside down...and still floating!

It takes more than we think to sink a lifeboat. It takes more than we think to sink a Church of Jesus Christ that takes the risk and rows back to rescue men, women, and children who are sinking without a Savior.

The only problem is this: We do not have enough lifeboat churches willing to row back

in the confidence that God will keep their lifeboat ship-shape.

Questions:

1. What got your attention in this chapter and what might God be trying to say to you through it?

2. What is your reaction to the opening prayer found at the beginning of this chapter?

3. What is your reaction to the stories of the lifeboats not wanting to go back to see if they could save some of the people in the water?

4. What do you legitimately fear if your church gets heavily involved in trying to rescue people who need saving?

5. What do you think of the fortress mentality?

CHAPTER FIVE
We Are Saved, *continued*...

But Jonah was greatly displeased and became angry (because the Lord showed compassion on Nineveh). He prayed to the Lord, "O Lord, is this not what I said when I was still at home? That is why I was so quick to flee to Tarshish. I knew that you are a gracious and compassionate God, slow to anger and abounding in love, a God who relents from sending calamity. Now, O Lord, take away my life, for it is better for me to die than to live."

Jonah 4:1-3

We have something; we feel guilty.

He was only 19. Far away from home. Fighting a war he didn't understand.

He was not alone.

As horrible as the whole experience was, there was one redeeming element. A friendship forged through fear and frustration. A friendship fired by a fight—a fight to stay alive.

"Incoming!" Someone yelled. Darkness exploded with light. Men casually shooting the breeze one moment were now diving for cover.

The 19-year-old...far away from home...fighting a war he didn't understand...was playing chess with his friend. They say you do not hear the shot that kills you. The 19-year-old heard the terrible explosion—he was alive. His friend, presumably, did not hear it—he was dead.

Upon returning to the States, the 19-year-old tried to make a go at living. He didn't make out so well.

I met him 17 years ago. Not long after I met him, I officiated his funeral. He died of an overdose of heroin.

His friends told me that he could never get over the guilt—the guilt of being alive.

———

He was only 17...far from home...clinging to an upside down lifeboat in the middle of the Atlantic. He was not alone.

Young Jack Thayer had made a friend in Milton Long during the supper hour of April 14, 1912. Only seven hours later they found themselves standing on the starboard side of the listing *Titanic*. All the lifeboats were gone. Jack wanted to jump for it and swim to a distant lifeboat he could just make out. Milton wasn't ready for it.

They waited. At 2:15 a.m. the bow of the ship went under and with it a wave was generated. Jack and Milton saw the wave coming. They shook hands and jumped.

Jack Thayer was one of the lucky 30 who climbed onto Collapsible Boat B and lived to tell of the sinking of the *Titanic*. Milton Long was never seen again.

After the *Titanic* disaster, Jack Thayer graduated from the University of Pennsylvania and went into banking. Eventually, he returned to the University as treasurer and financial vice president. In 1945 Jack Thayer, *Titanic* survivor, killed himself.

Why? We will never know for sure. But two things we do know. We know Jack was despondent over a son's death in World War II. We also know that throughout his life he was haunted by the memory of the *Titanic* sinking.

Two events. The first he survived; his friend Milton did not. The second he survived as well; his son did not.

Could it be that the guilt of being alive when loved ones were dead was the thing that killed him?

A Vietnam vet and a *Titanic* survivor—both recipients of unearned, unexplained grace. Why didn't they respond to their good fortune with a passion for life? Both could have—perhaps, should have—died. Instead, both lived. Shouldn't they have been so overwhelmed with the gift of life they had received that they would be motivated to live their lives helping others? Couldn't they have found purpose in living, not just for themselves, but for their friend that didn't make it?

It is hard to understand if you haven't experienced it. It seems that if a person is saved through no merit of his own and others are lost, it is hard for the saved person not to feel guilty for his salvation. It is almost as if the saved person feels he has been saved at the expense of the other who was lost. And the guilt slowly, little by little, kills the saved one. As if balance is only achieved when all are lost.

If I may presume you to be in the lifeboat, let me ask: How did you get there? How did you come to Christ? Did you ultimately do it? No. It was God's grace. Did you earn it? No, God gave it to you.

> It is by grace you have been saved, through faith—
> and this not from yourselves, it is the gift of God—
> not by works, so that no one can boast.
> Ephesians 2:8 (NIV)

Now, if it is true that you and I are in the lifeboat called the Church only by the grace of God, how do we deal with that? How do we deal with the fact that we received grace and are saved, and our unbelieving neighbor or co-worker may not be?

Isn't it logical that we would respond to our good fortune with a passion for life? We could have—perhaps, should have—died without Christ. We have been saved—we are high and dry in a lifeboat. We should be so overwhelmed with the gift of life that we are motivated to live our lives, trying to share the life Christ gives, with others. We should respond with lives of gratitude and purpose. Gratitude for a dry seat; purpose in helping others into the dry seat next to us.

It's logical. But logic does not always prevail. Very few in the lifeboat called the Church are passionately responding to their gracious position by attempting to rescue those not in the boat.

Why not? Let me suggest that many of us are suffering from guilt.

"Me, feel guilty about being saved?" you ask. "I don't feel guilty."

Guilt is so damning that we dilute and disguise it with other more manageable emotions.

Pride. An effective escape from the guilt of receiving undeserved grace is to believe that somehow we did something to deserve our seat in the lifeboat and our neighbor up to this point has not. We, with a hint of condescension, hope he smartens up before it is too late.

Shame. An equally effective escape from the guilt of receiving undeserved grace is to balance things out with our neighbor and jump in the cold water with her. We don't deserve a lifeboat seat and so we will do whatever it takes to lose our seat.

Denial. Perhaps the most common escape from the guilt of being on the receiving end of grace when those around you aren't is to close your eyes to those around you.

Many of those fortunate enough to find themselves in a *Titanic* lifeboat in 1912 dealt with the 1,500 men, women, and children crying out for rescue from the freezing water by closing their ears and hearts to their cries.

At the British inquiry in London, Sir Cosmo Duff Gordon was asked many times: "Did it occur to you that with the room in your boat, (he was one of 12 people in a boat that could carry 40), if you could get to these people you could save some?" He evaded a direct answer many times but eventually said, "I have said that I did not consider the possibility—or rather I should put it that the possibility of being able to help anybody never occurred to me at all."

Okay let's understand this. You are in a boat that has 32 empty seats. There are 1,500 people crying out to be saved. In fact, this is the only sound floating across the water, and the thought of the possibility of saving some does not occur to you???

Maybe there was a time in your life that you really saw people in need of a Savior. Often, sadly, the longer you are in the lifeboat, the farther you row from the thousands in the water, the fainter the cries for a Savior become. *Titanic* survivors had only to put up with the mournful cries for at most a half an hour. Then it was quiet.

Denial, shame, pride—all effective measures in dealing with the guilt of undeserved grace. All effective in keeping lifeboats empty.

We have something; we take it for granted.

I was born in a lifeboat. I was raised in a lifeboat. I went to school in a lifeboat. Most everyone I knew was in the lifeboat. I understood the purpose of the lifeboat. I was mentored in the art of rowing a lifeboat, cleaning the lifeboat, fixing the lifeboat. As I matured, people in the lifeboat recognized my abilities as a crew member. I was given more responsibility. It was a proud day for my parents when I was finally given the tiller of a lifeboat—my first church as a fully ordained pastor.

I knew lifeboats. I did not know much outside lifeboats. I knew of the ocean called the world and I occasionally ventured out for a swim in its icy waters, but I always had the shelter of a dry lifeboat to return to. It is a secure feeling to know you have a place and have always had a place in the lifeboat. But I have not always fully appreciated my place in the lifeboat.

I often took my place in a dry lifeboat for granted. So did my fellow lifeboat passengers.

Saved people who take their salvation for granted soon take each other for granted as well. Soon the mission is forgotten. Without a mission, people fight. And the fight usually has nothing to do with the mission.

The 700 fortunate *Titanic* survivors, spread over 20 lifeboats, forgot their mission, too. They began to fight. Not about going back to save others. No, the number one issue in lifeboat after lifeboat was...are you ready for this? Smoking! In 1912 tobacco was not as popular as it later became. At the American investigation, Senator Smith asked Mrs. J. Stuart White if she wished to mention anything about the discipline of the crew. She exploded, "As we cut loose from the ship these stewards took out cigarettes and lighted them. On an occasion like that!"

It is embarrassing to admit the kinds of things we in church spend our time arguing and getting upset about. Most of it has nothing to do with the mission of the lifeboat church.

Let's face it. Most churches have rowed so far away from struggling people without Christ in their lives that the people in the church just don't hear the cries. If you're like me, in that you were born in a lifeboat that has already rowed a great distance from the needy, perhaps you never heard a cry for help outside your church. For the first 17 years of my life, I never once witnessed a rescue. In fact, for the first 17 years of my life, I never once witnessed an attempt at a rescue. Everybody I knew was in the boat.

The vast majority of Christians alive today have been, like me, born into it. Perhaps our lifeboats, our churches are too far from those who need saving.

We are reached and we fear outreach will un-reach us.
"All this church cares about is outreach." Over the years I have heard this complaint spoken by frustrated people

attending my church. To be fair to their complaint, my passion for those not in the boat can and has, at times, overridden my responsibly to shepherd the flock that has hired me. The reached have as much right to the care and concern of their pastor as the unreached.

I suspect, however, that some of these church members tend to think of this dilemma as an "either or" one. Either I serve the one group or the other. Time spent with the unreached is time taken from the reached. But I don't see it as "either or." I see it as "both and." I cannot serve either the one or the other; I must serve both, the reached and the unreached. When I serve the unreached it is an example to the reached. I am leading the way. And when I serve the reached, I am serving the very ones that are needed to do the bulk of the outreach. And if I serve them, but in the end they do not end up doing any reaching out, then how successful have I been in serving the reached?

In a very real way the measure of how well a pastor serves the reached of his congregation is seen in how his congregation reaches out.

We have something; we want more.

How many times has a Christian moved into my city, come to my church for a time, and then decided to stay or go based on one thing: What does this church do for me?

"I've decided not to join your church because my kid's friends go to another church," one parent tells me.

"We've decided to switch to a bigger church because they have more programs for kids," someone else explains.

"We like your worship, but you don't have a church building."

"I am all for outreach but what about my needs and the needs of my family?" (The person asking the question was raised in a Christian home, went to a Christian school, and now sends his kids there. He has never rescued a single person with the life-saving power of Jesus Christ.)

What is going on here? Church people find themselves in a lifeboat and are not satisfied. They already have more than those living without Christ and yet the prime motivation is for themselves.

"All this church cares about is outreach. What about me? I'm sick of milk; I want meat," he says with a tinge of righteous indignation in his voice.

I come back with a little righteous indignation of my own. "I will agree to give you all the meat you could possibly eat if that is what it would take for you to get with the life-saving program. How much meat do you need in order to sit, twiddling your thumbs, in the middle of the lifeboat?"

We have something; we think we deserve it.

It was another late board meeting at the church. We were going to try something new. Some, in this 75-year-old church that I was pastoring, never thought it would pass at the congregational meeting. But it did. The people said "yes" to the proposal to add a morning service that was more contemporary and "seeker-sensitive." This was 1986 and we had no seeker-sensitive models at that time.

As I said, the proposal passed. But now those that didn't like the change that the proposal entailed came out in full force to protect their church.

The problem was not just the addition of another service, but a change of time for the current morning service—a half an hour change. If you want to hear church people whine and cry, try changing the service time.

The Board was meeting and folks had arrived to voice

the objections—even though everyone already had a chance to speak up when the vote was taken. Some were just not going to accept "yes" for an answer.

Woman: Why are we doing this?

Pastor: Our church is full; we need to do something.

Woman: We could squeeze a few more in the front next to the pulpit.

Pastor: New people come late; they will not sit up in front of everyone.

Woman: Well why don't they come on time like we do?

Pastor: I don't know. That's just the way it is. I'm just glad they are coming at all.

Woman: Well if they want our benefits they will have to sacrifice for them.

Pastor: They, the newcomer, should do the sacrificing?

Woman: That's the question, isn't it? Who should sacrifice, us or them? After all we built the church; we paid for it.

This is where I wanted to scream. If God had that kind of attitude, where would you and I be? He sacrificed His only Son for us. We are the ones who are called to pick up our cross daily and follow Him.

What is the deal?

Perhaps the most infamous *Titanic* lifeboat was Lifeboat No. 1. Duff Gordon, his wife, and his personal secretary, Miss Francatelli, asked if they could get into the lifeboat (even though the order was "women and children

PHOTOGRAPH OF TITANIC SURVIVORS CLEARS UP A MYSTERY.

only"). Murdoch, the officer loading the boat, said, "Yes, get in." Two American men—Abraham Salomon and C.E. Henry Stengel—joined them.

Murdoch then added seven members of the crew and put Lookout George Symons in charge. As Lifeboat No. 1 was lowered, Murdoch said to Symons, "Stand off from the ship's side and return when we call you." Lifeboat No. 1 did not stand by. Lifeboat No. 1 rowed away—12 people in a boat that could hold 40.

When the *Titanic* went down, Lifeboat No. 1 was a couple hundred yards away. Fireman Charles Hendrickson said, "It's up to us to go back and pick up any one in the water."

No one said a word. Finally, Duff Gordon announced that they shouldn't go back—too dangerous. With his few words the matter was dropped. Lifeboat No. 1 rowed away from the 1,500 desperate, dying men, women, and children.

How could this happen? For me, this single event raises the most puzzling, unanswerable question of the whole *Titanic* tragedy. How can a lifeboat with more empty seats than occupied row away from people who are drowning? I get angry when I think about the people in Lifeboat No. 1. I wish they were alive so I could scream at them.

Then I realize they are alive. They sit in church every Sunday. I sometimes sit with them, too. Ouch.

We have friends; we don't need any more.

When my family and I moved to Vancouver, I wondered how we were going to plant a new church—a new church designed to get non-churched people into church.

Our house was in a new subdivision of about 150 homes. My wife and I prayerfully made a goal of reaching three families in our subdivision. Having had my fill of knocking on doors 16 years prior, we decided to just walk around the neighborhood. We thought maybe if we walked around seven days in a row and seven times on the seventh day maybe the houses would come tumbling down and we would get people into our church. One day, my wife, Marie, was taking our kids out for a walk when she met a neighbor walking with her kids. They talked and discovered that their husbands both played tennis, so they arranged a match. I met Dave for the first time on the tennis court and of course, in the interest of evangelism, I let him beat me.

After tennis, we were invited to their house and from there a friendship was formed. I called or did something with Dave every week. Dave and his family came to church. They liked it. Three years later, Dave's wife Collette became a deacon and Dave became instrumental in finding land for a future church building. I don't know when they signed on the dotted line of Christianity. I am sure they thought they signed it years before. (That's what 75 percent of the North American population thinks, too.) I just became a friend and tried to share with them, through that friendship, authentic Christianity.

When you think about it, isn't that what God did? When God wanted to share His love with lost, blind, needy people, what did He do? Did He send us a cute pamphlet outlining the four spiritual laws? Did He send us a believer's prayer we can recite? Did He send down an insurance form that we could sign and date? No, He became one of us. The Word of God's love became flesh and lived among us. God witnessed, reached out, evangelized, and discipled us by becoming one us.

And what did He do when He was with us? Look at Jesus' ministry. He spent three years eating, working, playing, and living with 12 men who, through that long process, became disciples. And He called these people His friends. That is what it is all about. Making friends. Who can't make a friend? Concentrate on making friends with non-churched folks and you will make disciples.

If you were to ask me what I have learned in all my years of church planting, I would say this: Those in the church who have gone out and made friends of non-churched people have made the most progress in making disciples. How smart you are or how doctrinally aware you are has very little to do with it.

And let me say something radical. Radical but true. If you have all the friends you need and they are all Christians, your chances of making disciples are slim to none. At best you will adopt a few people as projects that you will soon tire of. The only way to truly make disciples is to befriend them, to make them a part of your circle— the people you spend Christmas with, the people you go camping with, the people you invite to your birthday party. And if you already have enough friends you will not add another. You must lose an old friend to make room for a new one in your life. Most of us are just plain unwilling to make that sacrifice. But that, friends, is what the cross is all about—sacrificing what you love for someone who may, in the end, reject your love. That is what God did. That is maybe what it means to "deny yourself and pick up your cross" and follow Him.

Questions:

1. What got your attention in this chapter and what might God be trying to say to you through it?

2. How do you struggle with the fact that you have been saved through no effort of your own?

3. How long have you been part of a church? What of it do you take for granted?

4. Why is it easier to see what you need from the church than what those not in it need from the church?

5. How is your friend and family situation keeping you from making new friends with people that need saving? What can you do about it?

CHAPTER SIX
Are We Saved?

By their fruit you will recognize them. Not everyone who says to me, "Lord, Lord," will enter the kingdom of heaven, but only the one who does the will of my Father who is in heaven.

Matthew 7:20-21

Let me give you a hint of where I am going with this chapter so that you can decide if you want to come along.

If it is real, you share it. (If it is not, you won't.)

This is how I see things. Maybe this makes sense to you; maybe it doesn't. This chapter could be a bit painful. At times you may think I'm too judgmental. You're probably right. But I say let's be hard on ourselves for a bit. Let's face the ugly side. Perhaps you would like to face it with a bit more grace than I am going to supply. But perhaps what many of us need is a good intervention—to be hit over the head, hard, to snap us out of denial.

Let's begin with a question: If Christians have been rescued from the waters of death and have been given a dry seat in the lifeboat called the church, why don't most Christians make it a huge priority to help others occupy the empty seat next to them? After all, if it is real, you share it.

Maybe you think it is real for you but still you do not share it. If this is so, one of three possibilities seems likely.

First possibility

Could it be that you just don't know how to share your faith? I grew up in Grand Rapids, Michigan—the Jerusalem of a denomination called the Christian Reformed Church of North America. The Christian Reformed Church is a relatively small denomination of some 300,000 members. Though small, it has done some big things. Most notably, it conceived, funded, and supplied some of the key personnel that made the NIV (New International Version) possible. The NIV is probably the most popular translation of the Bible in the world today. Members of the Christian Reformed Church produced

Christian publishers like Zondervan, Eerdmans, and Baker Books.

I went to Christian Reformed Churches growing up. I went to Christian Reformed day schools. I went to a Christian Reformed College and Seminary.

The roots of the Christian Reformed Church go back to the Netherlands and then back to John Calvin and the Reformation. Reformed people are big on God's sovereignty and the covenant. We believe that we are God's people by His choice, His grace alone. We and our children. Because of what God has done of His own will, not ours, we now respond in thanksgiving to Him.

I believe this Reformed stuff. I believe it because I read it in the Bible. I believe I am saved by grace alone and that everything I do that is good is a response to what God, through His Son, has done for me. With this background in mind I couldn't understand why we, as a denomination, didn't share the grace of God with those who did not know it. Oh, we shared it with each other, but we rarely got out of the lifeboat to share it with others.

If we have been rescued on no merit of our own, purely because of God's grace through someone who reached down and fished us out of the water, why aren't we motivated to be used by God to do the same for others? It seemed to me that Reformed people should be extra responsive to sharing God's love since we recognize so well, how freely we received it.

In all my years growing up in the Christian Reformed Church, I never witnessed a witnessing, never heard anyone share their faith with a non-Christian, never saw a non-Christian become a Christian and then be baptized as an adult. How could this be? How could people who have been saved not hear the cries of those yet in the water and not reach out and grab a hold of some—just one?

I don't think it is because we were uncommitted, Biblically illiterate, uneducated, slothful workers in God's kingdom. Our denomination had colleges, Christian worldwide radio programs, Christian schools, worldwide missions, a relief agency. No one could accuse Christian Reformed people of being lazy or indifferent to God. So why weren't we scooping people out of the water? And maybe more to the point: Why wasn't I?

I decided it was because we just didn't know how. I knew I didn't. So, after my last year of high school, I went on a church program that sent young people out to work in a newly established church for seven weeks in the summer. I figured if I stepped out into the mission field, someone would show me how to reach people. All I knew is that one way or another I was going to do it.

Two weeks after I was sent to Ogden, Utah, I was knocking on someone's door to share my faith for the very first time.

Here is what I learned: Not knowing how to share Jesus Christ is not the real problem. If a person is motivated enough, he or she will learn how. If a person is motivated enough, he or she will leave no stone unturned trying to figure out how. If a person is motivated enough, he or she will just do it, whether they have figured out how or not. The problem is one of motivation, not know-how.

If you really believed you were high and dry in the lifeboat called the church and there were drowning people all around your boat, would you dare not attempt to rescue them with the lame excuse that you don't know how?

Let's think this through. If your life were in jeopardy, wouldn't you do whatever you could do to save it? The doctor says, "Cancer." You may not know much about cancer at the time but wouldn't you do all you could to learn? Wouldn't you stay up into the wee hours of the night trying to figure it out?

Why is it that when we are talking about the eternal destination of our neighbors and coworkers and friends who do not know Christ we shrug our shoulders, do nothing, and exempt ourselves from the whole deal by saying we just don't know how? Let's be done with this lame excuse.

If it is real, people will share it.

Second possibility

Most Christians simply do not understand what they have been saved from. As a teenager I was determined to learn how to share my faith. After two weeks of training in lifesaving in Ogden, Utah, another teen and I were sent out to knock on some stranger's door and save them. We were equipped with the four spiritual laws, our own 5-minute testimony, and the naiveté to do as we were told. We knocked on a door and as we waited I prayed. "Lord, please let there be no one home." The Lord did not grant my request. A fifty-year-old lady answered the door and invited us in. We talked—about the carpet, the green couch, the pictures on the wall. She got out some needlepoint she had been working on and we oohed and awed. Finally after 25 very long minutes we left—never once mentioning God.

In my bed that night I resolved before God and the host of heaven to make up for my shame and share my faith the next day whether it killed me or not. At the door of a new house, on a new day, a Latino lady and her three preschool children met us. Because some beans were in the process of being refried, we congregated in her kitchen and it was there that I did what I was resolved to do. I shared a version of the four spiritual laws (Evangelism Explosion) that assumes you are hung up with earning your own salvation. When the "sharing the gospel" mission was completed, we left amidst the crying of kids and the stench of burning beans.

I remember lying awake that night thinking, "This is no way to reach people." I came to a stranger's house, interrupted her life, and gave her an answer to a question about grace I assumed she was asking. I didn't care enough about her to get to know her, to find out who she was and what her needs were. For all I knew her husband may have just left her and the biggest concern in her life was how she was going to put food on the table, not whether a person can earn her way to Heaven. I treated her as a client to whom I was trying to sell an eternal life insurance policy—the goal being to have her sign on the dotted line.

As I reflect back on this experience I realize that, not only did I not explore her need for a Savior, but I did not share my need for a Savior either. I shared what I had been taught to share—the four spiritual laws—what someone else had, perhaps had a passion to share. I did not share how Jesus became my Savior.

But to tell you the truth I'm not sure I would have known what to say if you had asked me why I needed a Savior back then. Oh, I could have told you that as one born in sin and thus deserving of eternal Hell, I needed someone who is God (being capable) and at the same time man (since man owed) to pay the debt of my sin. I could have then talked about Jesus as the God/man that meets these criteria. In short I could have explained that I needed a Savior to save me from Hell.

I believe there is a Hell. I believe if it were not for my Savior Jesus Christ I would end up in Hell. I believe my neighbor at this point in his life, from my human point of view, is headed for Hell. But I'm not that motivated to warn him about where he is headed and share how I am avoiding it.

Why? I suspect it is because I've never been to Hell. I don't know anyone that has been to Hell. If I had been dangling over the fires of Hell—literally—and then Jesus came and brought me to a cooler place I would do anything including hauling my neighbor out of his easy chair and dragging him to church. There would be passion in my concern for him. I would lose sleep trying to figure out how I could make Hell real for him. I would be on my knees praying hard that his heart would be softened to the gospel.

Now I am not saying I have no concern for my neighbor. I am just saying my being saved from Hell, though an intellectual surety, does not move me to share.

If it is real, you share it.

It was my first A.A. meeting. I was early. The guy who invited me had not yet arrived. I stayed in my car. "I'm not doing this alone." He arrived. Saw me. Waved me over. Before walking in to the meeting, he leaned over and whispered, "If anyone asks you a question, just say 'pass.'" I nodded. We headed in.

Three months earlier I had read a book about Dr. Bob, one of the cofounders of A.A.—Alcoholics Anonymous. Fascinating stuff. I read the Big Book—The Bible of A.A. I was amazed to discover that the Twelve Steps seemed to come straight out of the Bible. I decided to preach a series on the Twelve Steps and demonstrate how many of the principles of A.A. are found in the Bible. I asked those in recovery groups to help me. That's how I got to be invited to my first A.A. meeting.

I walked in confidently, knowing I could guard myself from any embarrassment with a simple word, "pass." Upon entering the meeting room an early-comer who was making coffee turned around and said, "Hi, I'm Dave, who are you?" Responding with the word "pass" did not seem appropriate. Besides, the meeting hadn't officially started yet, so I said, "Steve, glad to meet you." I thought, "no radical self-exposure here." But then came his follow up question. "Is this your first meeting?" Once again the word "pass" did not seem appropriate. Besides, what could be the harm in answering? "Yes it is."

Big mistake. When the others arrived, word got around like wild fire that I was a first timer. My purpose in being there was just to observe and to learn a few things so I could better preach about the Twelve Steps. I wanted to be anonymous (pun intended). Because I was a first-timer I became the focus of the whole meeting. One by one the guys in this group shared what it was like for each of them at their first meeting and then assured me they knew how I felt. I wanted to shrink into a hole. I didn't have the heart to tell them I was just a pastor passing through.

They opened their hearts to me. They talked about the fear, the loneliness, the guilt, the feelings of worthlessness, the emptiness, and the weariness. Many mentioned God, some their "higher power." One guy went on and on about how he never would have made it and never could make it without God in his life. After the meeting he came up to me and, not knowing I was a pastor whose job was to talk about God, said, "Don't sweat the God stuff." I said "okay" and thanked him for sharing with me.

One thing I learned that night: A.A. folks have no trouble sharing from what and how they were saved. They do not need external motivation. When they meet someone suffering from the affects of alcohol—something they have been saved from—nothing could stop them from sharing the hope that is in them. No courses in outreach are needed. No big "Each One, Reach One" campaigns. No "Bring a Drunk" Sundays. No public speakers on national TV trying to convince people of their drinking problems. No buildings. No paid staff. No seminaries. Just ordinary people from every walk of life; people who were slaves to alcohol and, through the help of people who once were slaves, have been shown the way to freedom.

They know precisely what they have been saved from. They know the pain and the hurt. They also know what being saved is like. When they meet someone who needs saving, they share with a passion. They share any way they can. They share because they have something that has truly affected their lives for the good.

In the Church we often try to force outreach. The church is not growing. So we set up an evangelism committee. The committee introduces the church to some program. But outreach programs designed to help people share their faith don't often last. Two months later most of those who took the course no longer use what they learned. It doesn't come from their experience.

You need something personal to share—something specific that you have been saved from. "I need Jesus in my life because _____." Whatever you put in the blank has to come from your heart if it is going to make an impact when you share it.

So the critical questions are:
How have you experienced the Savior?
What has Jesus Christ saved you from?
And, how did it happen?

If it is real, people will share it.

Where in your life did you finally give up trying to control things and give control to Jesus? Where did your spiritual poverty and Jesus' spiritual wealth meet? In what area of your life were you dead, but now are alive because of the resurrection power of Jesus?

Step 12 of A.A. reads: "Having had a spiritual awakening as the result of these Steps, we tried to carry this message to alcoholics, and to practice these principles in all our affairs."

The critical phrase here is "Having had a spiritual awakening." How does Jesus in your life make you alive, awake? If you are fuzzy about the answer to this question, why should the person you are trying to share Christ with want Christ in his or her life? If all you do is share Christ in vague generalities and philosophical arguments, is it any wonder that you don't lead many people to Christ?

You have to share your heart and your soul with its brokenness, and your need for the healing power of Jesus. You are not just sharing a static set of propositions. You are sharing a relationship that you have with a person. And the relationship you have with the person Jesus Christ is one that grows, changes, and has its ups and downs. There is no safe, unexposed way to share your faith. You must share your story.

Okay, I just said you must share your story. But the truth is, you will share your story, your relationship to

Jesus. You cannot help it. But, if your relationship to Jesus is impersonal, that is how you will share Him. If your relationship is a vague set of propositions, that is how you will share it. Of course your opportunities to share a vague set of propositions won't come too often. If your relationship to Christ consists mainly in how you live your life, that is what you will, with some passion, share with others. If your relationship to Christ is largely the ritual of going to church every Sunday, your outreach strategy will, for the most part, be one of inviting the occasional person to church. If your relationship to Christ is largely one of study, reasoning and argument, you will tend to engage people that want to debate with you. If your relationship with Jesus is an intimate roller coaster of emotion, that is how you will communicate Jesus with others. If your relationship with Jesus is intertwined in your relationship to your spouse, you will probably advocate Jesus as the marriage builder.

Do you get what I am saying? Wherever you are in your relationship to Jesus—whatever form that takes—that is what and where you will most passionately share Him.

———

During my first year of college I was wrestling with God's grace and our moral responsibility. I couldn't understand the relationship between doing good and grace. If I am saved totally by God's grace, apart from works, then why should I do good? On the other hand, when I went to church the pastor was always challenging us to live this way or that, in short: to do good. But do I have to? After all, my goodness does not contribute to my salvation.

Then I read the story of the Prodigal Son. The son in effect wishes his father dead when he takes his inheritance and goes to the big city. He blows his money and has nowhere to turn. He is hungry and he thinks of the food his father's servants have. He wants to go back. But how? He has offended his father. He will go back and say that he is sorry. Why? Because he wants something.

He goes home. His father has been waiting for him. His father humiliates himself in front of the whole village by running to meet his wayward son. Next comes the part I had never noticed before. The father throws his arms around his son *before* his son opens his mouth. The father's love is spontaneous and unconditional. It is not dependent on the son's confession. The son does confess. He says, "Father I have sinned against heaven and against you…" But notice, the confession comes after he is unconditionally received, not before. His confession is a response to his father's love, not the condition for it.

I finally understood God's grace. I had a new relationship with Him. Yes, it was still a very intellectual kind of relationship but that is where I was. I was saved from intellectual confusion about God's love. And you know what? I couldn't help share what had happened. I worked the story of the Prodigal Son into every single paper that I had to write that year—a history paper, an English paper, a psychology paper, a sociology paper, and even a music paper. I just couldn't help it.

If it is real, you share it.

So if you want to know what kind of relationship you have with Jesus, pay close attention to how you share him.

My guess is that many Christians have kind of a family hand-me-down relationship with Jesus. We are just doing what our parents did with us. We know the right words; we do the right things. We share Christ, but only in the lifeboat. Perhaps this is a relationship to Christ, but it certainly isn't a very close one.

If our faith in Jesus Christ is real but there is little evidence of that in terms of rescue attempts, perhaps we need to take our relationship with Christ to another level.

Try to answer these two questions:
In what specific areas of your life has the Savior saved you?
In what specific areas of your life do you still need a Savior?

Third possibility
The third possibility of why a person in the church lifeboat might not seem to be actively scooping people out of the waters of eternal death, is that the person is mistaken about his or her place in the lifeboat.

In the Old Testament, the prophet Amos had to warn people who thought they were in the lifeboat:

Woe to you who are complacent in Zion, and to you who feel secure on Mount Samaria, you notable men of the foremost nation, to whom the people of Israel come!

Amos 6:1

In the New Testament, Jesus had to warn people who thought they were in the lifeboat:

*Not everyone who says to me, "Lord, Lord," will
enter the kingdom of heaven, but only he who does
the will of my Father who is in heaven.*

Matthew 7:21 (NIV)

If it is real, you share it.
If you do not share it, it is not real.

Bruce Ismay, the president of the White Star Line, was
onboard the maiden voyage of the *Titanic* and helped load
passengers into the lifeboats. He learned directly from Captain Smith, 30 minutes after the
collision with the iceberg, that the
Titanic was finished. He helped
load Collapsible Boat C, one of the
last remaining boats. And, just before it was lowered, he jumped in.

Captain Smith went down
with the ship. Thomas Andrews,
the architect of the *Titanic* went
down with the ship. John Jacob

Bruce Ismay

Astor, one of the world's richest men alive at that time,
went down with the ship. Bruce Ismay did not go down
with his ship. He was saved. Or was he? Bruce Ismay
never did recover. His remaining years were spent in seclu-
sion. He died a bitter, broken man. In many ways, Bruce
Ismay did in fact go down with the ship.

Why? Because he could not share his seat in the lifeboat with the 1,500 people who went down with the ship.

If you do not share it, perhaps it is not real.
Questions:
1. What got your attention in this chapter and
    what might God be trying to say to you

through it?

2. In what specific areas of your life has the Savior saved you?

3. In what specific areas of your life do you still need a Savior?

4. How have you shared your faith with others? What does that tell you about your faith?

CHAPTER SEVEN
Capsized Clergy

*"Ladies, if any of us are saved, remember I
wanted to go back. I would rather drown with
them than leave them."*

Seaman Jones

Officer Lightoller put Seaman Jones in charge of Lifeboat No. 8. When the *Titanic* sank, Jones, as the leader, made the call to go back and try to rescue some of the 1,500 who were in desperate need of a lifeboat. But those with him in Lifeboat No. 8 were against the idea.

Seaman Jones clearly heard the cries of those in the water and the cries of those in the boat. He could not respond positively to both.

If you are a pastor or a leader in a church, God has put you in charge of a lifeboat. You hear the cries of those who have not yet experienced the lifechanging power of Christ. You see people in the neighborhood, in stores, in the workplace, people all around you that are floundering in the black waters of despair. I have to believe that you want to make rescue attempts.

Many pastors I know agonize about the brokenness that they see. They want to row back. They talk about rowing back. But you know what? Most don't.

Why?

Lack of training

Pastor Bob dreamed of being a pastor his whole life. He dreamed of using his God-given gifts to advance the Kingdom of God. Wanting to be the best that he could be, he enrolled in seminary. He learned to read the New Testament in the original Greek. It required more discipline than he had ever needed before, but his dream to pastor was strong. He learned, to a lesser degree, to read some of the Old Testament from the original Hebrew. He studied theology in all its many facets. He applied his learning to practical pastoral activities like preaching and teaching. He took counseling courses. In short, he spent three years learning how to meet the spiritual needs of those in the lifeboat.

How about those outside the lifeboat? Well he did take one course in evangelism. But all they did in class was talk about evangelism. No one actually went out and did it.

Bob was confident about taking care of the people in the lifeboat but had no clue how to go after people in the water.

Okay, I am not talking about Bob. I am talking about myself. I had no clue how to go after people in the water. I wasn't trained. No one ever helped me or forced me to get out there and do it.

Excuses. Nothing but excuses. How much training does it take to grab an oar and start rowing? There may be better ways to row, there may be better ways to reach out and drag people into the boat, but most anything you do is bound to have some positive result. It's doing something—anything—that counts.

As I said before, not knowing how to do something is never a good excuse because if you really believe in something and really want to do it, you will learn how.

Lack of the gift of evangelism

You are not a salesman. You are a pastor—you respond to those whom you already know would appreciate a visit. They won't reject you. They will welcome you and thank you for your visit. You are a preacher—you speak to a group of people that gratefully gives you the floor and their attention. You don't have to win the microphone or sell your thoughts to get it.

Rejection. That is what most pastors fear. Do my church members like my preaching? Do they appreciate my pastoral care? Are they following my leadership? Do they like me? Evangelism is too much like selling a vacuum cleaner to somebody that really doesn't want a vacuum cleaner. The likelihood of rejection is great.

And because you, the pastor, feel like you are not good at evangelism, how can you encourage, challenge, and lead the charge in the area of evangelism?

Lack of incentive

Why would a pastor be motivated, from the human perspective, to row back? Who pays the pastor's salary? Who can make things go well or not go well for the pastor? It is the people in the boat. If, as a pastor, I were to visit a non-churchgoing person in the community, who really is going to care? If, on the other hand, I visit a grandmother of one of the ladies in my church, my praises would be sung at the next ladies society meeting.

Lack of courage

Most pastors simply lack the courage to face the people in the boat who fear rowing back for all the reasons we talked about in previous chapters. In fact, many pastors lack the personal courage to simply go back themselves, or at least call the people to go back.

Lack of boldness

Seaman Jones wanted to row back and try to save those in the water. In fact, he let everyone in his boat know that he personally would be willing to sacrifice his life to make the rescue attempt. "Ladies, if any of us are saved, remember I wanted to go back. I would rather drown with them than leave them," he is reported to have said. He had boldness in words but not in action.

Many pastors talk about evangelism—with some passion—but when it comes to boldly rowing in the direction of the lost, regardless of how the church they are leading feels about it, many pastors fail to do it.

Lack of ownership in the lifeboat

Perhaps the real problem in the church is that most pastors are not the real pastors of the church. Many pastors are simply paid chaplains hired to serve the lifeboat members. Many pastors are just dedicated servants doing the bidding of those who hired them. Some understand they are called to be more than hired hands, so they at least give lip service to the call to row back. And when the church as a whole complains, "All we talk about is the lost around here. What about us longtime church members?" the pastor loudly proclaims that "when Jesus comes back I want it known that I would rather be lost with those outside the church than not try to save them." Words, but no action.

Lack of leadership

Though Seaman Jones had the training and the tiller, he was not the leader of Lifeboat No. 13. If he was the leader, he would have led and the people in the boat would have had to follow. Why? Because a true leader has followers. We have a saying around our church: If you are a leader, show me your group. Seaman Jones had a title; he had the megaphone, but when leadership was needed no one looked to him.

Many pastors have the title. They have the pulpit

every Sunday. They may even have the tiller at the board meetings. But many of those same pastors are not true leaders.

When I became a pastor fresh out of seminary I took the helm of a 70-year-old church of 450 people. They made me president of the board. I spoke to attentive crowds every Sunday morning and night. I thought I was the leader.

Think this through. The members grew up in this church. Their parents built it. Most will one day be wheeled down the center aisle for their last sermon prior to the graveyard. This is their church—this is their small part of the body of Christ. I was hired to help them manage it. To use the business metaphor, they were the stockholders, I was the portfolio manager. If I had known what I am now talking about back when I started in ministry, I wouldn't have been surprised at the push-back I got when I put drums in the church, or tried to go to a second morning service, or hired the first secretary the church ever had, or—horror of all horrors—suggested that we change the time of the morning service.

Leaders lead. Seaman Jones had the tiller. He had the authority. He should have said, "We are rowing back. That is what lifeboats do. You may not like it, but that is what we are going to do. And you will have to throw me out of the boat to stop it from happening." By the way, I did manage to put drums in the church, go to a second morning service, hire the first secretary, and change the morning service time. And there were some people in the church who tried to throw me out of the boat. But guess what? The church I was leading was not my church. The church was not their church either. The church was the Lord's church. And He had plans for His church, that it would extend His love to those He had in mind.

Questions:

1. What got your attention in this chapter and what might God be trying to say to you through it?

2. If you are a pastor, which of these "lacks" in this chapter do you lack?

3. If you are a church member, you are called to be a leader as well. Which of these "lacks" can you relate to?

4. In your church, how much does the pastor lead and how much do the few certain people who have been in the church for a long time lead?

5. How much emphasis does the leadership put on evangelism?

PART TWO
Why Aren't There Enough Lifeboats (Churches)?

Why plant churches?

- For every church that opens, four close.
- 65% of Americans have no church contact whatsoever.
- The United States has the fourth largest population of unreached in the world. Only India, China, and Malaysia have more unreached than here.
- Church attendance has declined 19.4% in the last 10 years.
- 85% of all churches in America are either plateaued or in decline.
- Of the 15% that are growing, 85% are doing so by transfer growth. That means…only 1 out of 100 churches are winning the lost to Christ.
- Only 28% of ages 23-37 attend church.
- Statistics show that church plants are 16 times more effective at winning converts than established ones.

Why plant churches? …that is why.

New Breed Church Planting
www.newbreedcp.org

CHAPTER EIGHT
The Cruise Ship Mentality

*For the time will come when people will not put
up with sound doctrine. Instead, to suit their
own desires, they will gather around them a great
number of teachers to say what their itching ears
want to hear.*

2 Timothy 4:3

In the winter of 2003, to mark our 25th anniversary, I took my wife Marie on our first cruise. Well, I didn't actually take her. My parents were celebrating their 50th wedding anniversary and took all of their children and spouses with them. Lucky for me, our 25th anniversary just happened to coincide with their 50th.

I had never been on a big ship before. It was overwhelming. Unbelievable. There was the food—all you could eat, anything you wanted. Add to that the entertainment—shows, sports, song and dance. And then the ports of call—excursions, the beach, and the ocean. On top of all this there was the fun of being together—laughing, singing, and playing. In short, our cruise was a wonderfully self-indulgent, first-class experience.

Even though we went on this cruise six years after the movie *Titanic* came out, we all, with child-like excitement, went to the bow of the ship and took turns striking the "I'm king of the world!" pose. (In the movie, Jack stands behind Rose at the very bow of the ship, takes her two hands, and raises them until she is standing with her arms outstretched on each side). The pictures we took weren't quite as romantic, but we had fun making fun of each other.

All in all it was a great vacation. It was our getaway. It was about our happiness and pleasure. It was not about those we left behind. It was not really about helping people. It was not about making great things happen in the world. It was not about making a difference. It was about us—our fun, our time, and our relaxation. This is the cruise ship mentality.

In 1912 there were no cruise ships. The *Titanic* was a passenger ship. Its main purpose was to take passengers from point A to point B. Trips were one-way and the goal was the destination. Folks back then never would have dreamed that people would one day be taking a passenger ship that would start at point A and seven days later bring the same people back to point A. With a cruise ship, it is not the final destination that matters, but the fun along the way.

White Star Line was a passenger ship liner, with a dream of becoming more with the building of three sisters ships that were quite unlike any ship built before—the *Olympic*, *Titanic*, and *Gigantic* (after the sinking of the *Titanic* they renamed this third ship, *Britannic*). They were the first passenger ship

> *Nothing has been omitted in the determination to place the two new White Star leviathans beyond criticism as to the excellence of the accommodation both in the second and third classes…the spaces provided for second class promenades are unusually spacious…the boat deck is surmounted only by the open canopy of heaven.*
>
> White Star Line

liner to start thinking not only about the destination, but the experience along the way. And nothing illustrates this more to me than the boat deck. This was the top deck from which passengers, each class with their own section, could walk in the open, to gaze at the endless sky against the deep blue sea. The managers of the *Titanic* experience were so keen on its passengers getting a first-class experience that they made a fateful decision concerning the boat deck. It had to do with the number of lifeboats.

There weren't enough lifeboats for all on the *Titanic*. At capacity this new ship could hold just over 3,000 people. Legally, *Titanic* needed lifeboats for just over 1,000. Explanation: In 1912, the *Titanic* was the culmination of

a 20-year period of phenomenal growth in the passenger ship industry. Ships went from 5,000 tons to 45,000 tons during these few short years. The rules governing lifeboats were based on tonnage (with 15,000 tons the upper limit), not people.

Interestingly enough, the designers of the *Titanic* went out of their way to build each lifeboat station so that each could accommodate four lifeboats, thus making it possible for a grand total of 48 lifeboats. Just before sailing, only 32 lifeboats were on board. At the last minute, those in authority at White Star Line thought that so many lifeboats on the boat deck would cheapen the first class experience they wanted to give their passengers. Besides, with the innovation of watertight compartments in the hull of the ship, lifeboats were deemed practically irrelevant. So 12 lifeboats were off-loaded.

It was the cruise ship mentality of the White Star Line with regard to the boat deck that ultimately lead to the loss of so many people in the icy waters of the Atlantic.

The cruise ship mentality is about the journey, not the destination; it is about fun, not purpose; it is the customer and his first class experience, not the needs of those outside the ship. And, I am afraid to say, for fear of what some of you readers are going to think, it is about being big—even *Titanic*—not small. Let me take that back. It is not about being big; it is simply that "big" seems to be a necessity for success with the cruise ship mentality.

Most churches across North America are not big and certainly not a first class experience—a cruise ship. Most are small—with 120 members or less. They are short staffed with an inconsistent set of volunteers. They generally need new carpet, or a repaved parking lot, or a copy machine, or something else necessary for ministry—usually something they cannot afford. And, contrary to what most people think, the average church plant has only 120 people after four years. And most people in them are tired of setting up chairs in a rented space every week and desperately want a place of their own. Some go for it and then end up with a dream-crushing mortgage to contend with.

No, most churches across North America are not cruise ships, but—and here is the point—they want to be, or at least they think they have to be to attract new members. And this thinking has a negative impact on church planting.

Okay, I can already feel some of you getting your guard up. It seems I am equating large church with cruise ship mentality. And you sense that the cruise ship mentality isn't going to be a good thing. Indulge me. You can have a small church with the cruise ship mentality and I suppose you can have a large church that doesn't have the cruise ship mentality. Maybe you are in a large church with great, sincere people being led by Christ-like servant leaders. And maybe your church is really trying to reach out to those in the water. All that said, I think there is just a plain and simple danger with size. Even if your church is one of the large churches that is on a good track, the unintentional wake produced by your church may be causing little lifeboat churches to capsize—and your church is not even aware of it. I think the large church and the example of the large church to the small church lends itself to several cruise ship related problems—problems that ultimately affect church planting. Maybe I am being unfair and overly simplistic, but I think there are a few challenges to consider. At least hear me out. You can always disagree.

Challenge One: Personal Choice

We were all sitting around the fire in the dark. It was a big group for a fire but a very small group for classmates celebrating their 25th high school anniversary. My wife graduated from a small Christian school in Seattle, Washington—just 24 students. It was fun to listen to these long time friends reminisce about the four years they spent in school together. You could tell they were close, that they shared something special, that they were family in some way. With only 24 students there wasn't an abundant array of classes and specialized opportunities. They had to get by with limited resources. They had to compromise. They were too small to have programs catering to each one's exact needs. But the lack seemed to bond them together. It reminded me of stories I heard as a kid about the one room schoolhouse. Classmates had to help each other. School was as much about community as it was about learning. And lines between being taught and teaching were somewhat blurred.

Sounds like what the church should be, doesn't it?

My wife graduated with a class of 24. My two oldest sons graduated from a school of 4,000. There was a program for every conceivable interest. Our sons had a lot of options. Many choices. They could do whatever they liked. But I am not sure they will ever have a 25-year reunion around the fire.

B.H.F. Before Henry Ford, the church you went to was the one you could walk to. The community you lived in was, for better or worse, your church.

A.H.F. After Henry Ford, people could drive to whatever church they liked. What a person liked, in terms of church, became part of the equation. Today, when people look for a church they look for one they like. Driving by one church to go to another. Finding a preacher that they like—one that informs, inspires, and makes them laugh. Programs for the children. Something for the wife and husband. A few missional experiences in foreign countries for excitement and a sense of purpose. Variety. An a la carte menu (you can be as involved as you want to be). Anytime seating. Show-like, quality services. All at an affordable price.

Sounds a lot like a cruise ship doesn't it?

Churches grow big because people like them. In a big church you hear people say:

I *like* the programs.

I *like* the pastor.

I *like* the sermons.

I *like* the music.

I *like* the specialized interest group that is into the exact thing that I am into.

Okay, let me ask you. Where is the focus in "I like?" Do you see the problem?

I rarely hear people say as they join a church, "I know

this church has a lot of needs and problems. That is why I feel called to come here—to use my gifts and abilities to help this church fulfil its mission in this place." When members leave a church to join another don't they usually talk about what they don't *like* in the one they're leaving, and what they do *like* in the one they are joining? Shouldn't they be talking about where they feel called regardless of what they like or don't like?

So, big churches become big because people like them. Big churches become even bigger because big churches (since they are big) are able to create better programs in more areas that more and more people like. The more programs there are, the more likely it is that there will be a program to meet each member's unique needs and interests.

Some of you are thinking, "So what? What is the problem with a church developing more and better programs to meet more members' unique needs and interests?" Think back to my example of the big versus the little school. More and better is not always better. In the large church there is so much geared toward you, the member, that it is hard not to think the church is all about you—the church member—and your needs and interests. And the reason this is more of a problem in a large church is because a large church has the potential to develop many and more specific programs to meet many and more specific needs and interests. In a small church, not unlike the one room schoolhouse, everyone has to compromise because there aren't enough people to create a lot of different programs. A few programs must fit all.

Not convinced? When someone caters to your every need, it's hard not to feel a sense of entitlement. Look at some of our young professional sport stars. Look at kids whose parents try to constantly please them. Look at, dare I say, Christian Youth Ministry. Over the past 20 years the church in North America has invested more resources into the youth of our churches than at any other time in church history. Money, mission trips, paid youth pastors, special worship services designed by and for the youth, and on and on. And yet study after study suggests that some 60 percent of these same youth, who have been catered to all their church lives, leave the church and don't come back. And when asked why they are leaving the church, they say things like, "I don't like it. It doesn't meet my needs." Why are we surprised? We have catered to our youth. We have tried to create a church youth environment that fits their needs exactly. They haven't had to learn how to compromise for the sake of others. They haven't had to learn to be satisfied by being just one group in a church that consists of many groups. To meet their specific needs, we have isolated them into their own special interest group. We have taught them that church is all about them and then we are surprised that they leave the church for other secular opportunities that promise to make them happy.

My point here is not about the youth. What has happened to our youth is just an example of what we are now doing to the rest of the church. And all I'm saying is a church needs to be big in order to really cater to the needs of all members. But, catering to all members' needs produces self-indulgent members who never learn to compromise for the sake of others.

Challenge Two: Shopping for a Church
When someone caters to your every need it is hard not to look around to see who can cater better—to shop for that which will meet your unique needs and accommodate

your unique interests. With regard to church, we call it "church shopping."

Back in 2003 when my wife and I took our first cruise, we thought the food, the room, the entertainment, the décor, the staff—all of it was incredible. A couple years later we took a second cruise on a different cruise line. The first thing we did, without even thinking about it, was compare. "The piano player isn't as good is he? The food? I like the frozen yogurt this one has, but I'm not sure about the dining." At dinner we ate with people we hadn't previously met. The questions everyone asked each other were, "Have you cruised before? What cruise line? How was it?" I never heard so much complaining by people who were at the height of living it up. You see, once you are in an environment that caters to your every need, it's hard not to become self-absorbed. Once you are self-absorbed, you become a shopper.

Personal choice leads to a shopping—or what we often call the consumer attitude or mentality. It's all about what people want. Churches create products (worship, education, outreach, pastoral care, congregational life, etc.). Churchgoers then shop around to find out which church has the products they want. Then these churchgoers buy into that church's products with their time and money. The process is really clear and business like. Result: The churches that produce what most people want will grow.

Shopping can be fun for the shopper. But it's not so much fun for the store owner. From the store owner's perspective, shopping makes store ownership very competitive. "You check my store out and then you compare it with someone else's store. The store that best meets your perceived needs gets your business. I must compete with every store."

In a church shopping culture, each church must compete for customers. If a church doesn't compete, it goes out of business. Of course, we never talk about this because we all know that Jesus is the head of one body. Though this body manifests itself in many parts (different denominations; different local churches), all of these parts make up the one Church of Jesus Christ. Christianity is not about my church or your church—we're in this together. And ultimately, if my church gains members and your church loses members, we all lose.

But I doubt that growing churches lose much sleep over churches that go out of business. They don't have time to. They are too busy trying to manage their own church.

This business of church shopping makes churches competitors. And this competitive nature between churches comes out in very subtle and interesting ways. For example, when a successful, growing church loses their pastor there's an intense search to find an above-average replacement. Why not? A lot rides on whether a church has a great pastor or an average one. Let's say the church searching for an above-average pastor finds one. This is great news for that church, but it means another church doesn't get that above-average pastor. They, perhaps, must settle for an average pastor. I mean, there are, by definition, only so many above-average pastors. Most pastors are average. That is what average means. Perhaps, to be fair to the whole body of Christ, if one church has enjoyed an above-average pastor for many years, it should take its turn with an average pastor—let some other church enjoy a little success.

Most pastors I know have a heart for the unity of the body of Christ. They really do. But what can pastors do in the face of the consumer-based, shopping mentality that drives church membership these days?

Challenge Three: The stratification and breakup of the family

I was at a big church planting conference in Orlando, Florida. There must have been 4,000 church planters, denominational leaders of church planters, and want-to-be church planters running around looking for some secret, some insight, some concept, or some connection to something that would help them to become better church planters.

I wanted to be inspired, but in the end I found it depressing. Sitting in the hall of the main auditorium, I overheard a church planter talking about how great his church plant was going—thousands of people coming in just a few years. Wow. Then I heard him say that Chris Tomlin (one of today's most well-known Christian artists) is the worship leader at his church. How reproducible is that? Another guy told a pastor that he knew this famous professional basketball player. The pastor asked, "Would he be willing to come to my church and give a little talk? Of course we pay pretty good for that kind of thing."

That was it. I got up. I needed some air. I saw in my program that some famous guy who wrote a book was speaking in the building next door. "Well, I'm here," I thought. "Let's see what this is all about." As I walked into the atrium of this new building I was confronted with three-story facade of what looked like a cruise ship. This gigantic building was for the kids programs of the church. On it, in big letters was the word: DiscipleSHIP. Very clever. So, it turns out this conference was being held at a church that had literally constructed a cruise ship (at least a facade of one) to keep their young people interested.

Is this what is necessary to reach kids for Christ these days? Is this what we need to do to reach our own children?

Personal choice leads to shopping for the right church. Shopping for the right church for most families should lead them to look for a church that can come along side them as they seek to challenge and encourage and disciple their children in a walk with the Lord. In truth, most parents are looking for a church that will do the discipling for them.

The Sunday School

Sunday school was never intended to be a program for the children of the church. Did you know that? It began as a program to teach basic Christianity to the children of parents that didn't go to church. It was an outreach program. What about the church kids, the children of parents that went to church? Who was supposed to teach them? You probably guessed it. Parents.

> In the early days, what we now term religious education was primarily a function of the home. Parents were expected to train their children in knowledge of the Scriptures and also of the doctrines...It was the pastor's responsibility to see that this duty was not neglected.[2]

Over the last 200 years, Sunday school became the system of spiritual education for all children. And as Sunday school did more, it might be argued, the parents did less.

Many parents, instead of partnering with the Chil-

2. Ernest Trice Thompson, Presbyterians in the Sound, Volume One 1607-1861, p. 223.

dren and Youth Ministries of the church, let these programs shoulder most of the responsibility for the spiritual development of their own children. It becomes a vicious circle. The leaders in the church see that the parents are doing less and less and thus try to make up for it by having the church do more and more. But the more the church does, the less the parents do. Eventually church leaders burn out trying to make up for the basic Christianity that should be taking place in the home.

And this phenomenon of the "programs" taking over the responsibility that once was in the home is not just found in Sunday school.

Today, most churches operate like a mall. As a family, you go to the mall together. Everyone is excited. You are doing this together, as a family. You park the car. You walk in as a family. You get to the fountain. The parent then looks at his or her watch and says, "Alright, let's meet back here at three o'clock." Then, each family member goes to the store that best meets his or her needs and interests.

Families may still go to church together, but the church programs are so well-developed and tuned to the special needs and interest of each age group that families get divided up.

Isn't this what's happening in the secular world? Special interest groups are picking off our family members one by one. "So what?", you may say. Everyone is happy getting what he or she wants. I have my doubts about how happy everyone is. One thing I have no doubts about: When family members get to wallow in their own special interest, they never learn how to develop a family interest.

So, how does life go in our fragmented world? Dad

plays golf with his friends on Tuesdays, and he also meets with men from the church for Saturday morning Bible study. Mom has quilting club, and she's also in the Mom's Morning Out group at church. The daughter is on the school basketball team, and she's also in the church choir. Both sons play club soccer, and they're also part of the youth group at church. Now take this family, multiply the number of special interest groups they're in by five, and you'll start to see the picture. Families are being torn apart by all these special interest groups—both secular and church related.

So how is the church any different than the secular world we live in terms of pulling families apart?

Oh, by the way, there is one secular company that gets what I am talking about, perhaps better than the church does. Can you guess what company?

Disney. When Disney makes a movie, their goal is to bring families together to watch it. They have plenty of elements for the kids. But they also throw in elements that only the parents get.

Almost every organization, every product, is pulling families apart—each person to his or her own special interest. The church should be the organization that helps families stay together.

The Unintended Wake of the Cruise Ship Church

I was to preach at the small church that my younger brother attended. The leadership was thinking about shutting its doors. Over a 20-year period the membership never went above 100. Now it was 50.

My brother and sister-in-law were newly married with no kids so when they joined the church five years earlier, they volunteered to run the youth program. A mobile home park next to the church supplied plenty of interesting kids from some very interesting home situations.

As I said, the leadership was thinking about shutting the church down. The church had always struggled in its history—requiring help from the five large, neighboring sister churches in the same little town. The church never had a real positive view of itself, compared to "The Big Five." It was one of those churches from the wrong side of the tracks, just getting by, always in debt, needing help.

I wondered what I should say to this little church? So I did a little research into what we in our denomination call the Yearbook. I discovered that my brother's little church—this dependent, fragile group of people from the wrong side of the tracks—had reached more people for Christ (new people to the faith) than the five large churches combined.

The Big Five had bigger buildings, more impressive pastors, more and better programs than the little church, but when it came to getting people into the lifeboat, the little church won that competition hands down.

So why were the leaders of the little church talking about shutting down? Maybe they were tired of feeling like a second-class church. Maybe they were tired of just getting by and always needing help. Or maybe they were just tired of reaching people for Christ, discipling them in the Christian life, and encouraging them in their spiritual gifts only to have them enticed away to a bigger church with more bells and whistles.

No one intends for this to happen. No one in the bigger church would ever say that a small outreach church was second-class. When a bigger church lends a hand to a smaller church it honestly just wants to help. And when churchgoers from a smaller church come to believe their needs would be better met in a nearby larger church, is that church supposed to refuse them?

See, it's all unintentional. But the consequences of the big wake caused by the big church are still a reality.

Okay. Maybe you agree with some of what I have been saying about the cruise ship mentality. Maybe you disagree. Or maybe you have to think about it. But, agree or not, you must be wondering what all this has to do with the question posed in Part Two of this book: Why aren't there enough lifeboats (churches)? What does the cruise ship mentality have to do with this question?

I felt we really had to understand what the cruise ship mentality was before we applied it to our question. But now we are ready. Here it is: The cruise ship mentality keeps middle to semi-large churches from planting new churches.

I know several churches of 1,000 members or more that have never planted a church and do not feel ready to do so.

Someone once asked, "How big does a church have to be before it can successfully plant a church?"

The answer, "Just a little bit bigger."

Oh, there is one more thing. According to research done by Christian Schwarz (in his book *Natural Church Development*) small churches of 53 people or less are 16 times more effective in winning new converts to Christ than mega churches.

Questions:

1. What got your attention in this chapter and what might God be trying to say to you through it?
2. How does the cruise ship metaphor fit parts of your church?
3. How has the idea of "personal choice" affected your expectations of what church ought to do for you?
4. What do you think of church shopping?
5. How is your family being pulled about by everyone's special interests?
6. How is your church helping you take more responsibility for the faith in your own home?

CHAPTER NINE
The Fishing Boat Church Attitude

To some who were confident of their own righteousness and looked down on everyone else, Jesus told this parable: "Two men went up to the temple to pray, one a Pharisee and the other a tax collector. The Pharisee stood by himself and prayed: 'God, I thank you that I am not like other people—robbers, evildoers, adulterers—or even like this tax collector. I fast twice a week and give a tenth of all I get.' But the tax collector stood at a distance. He would not even look up to heaven, but beat his breast and said, 'God, have mercy on me, a sinner.'"

Luke 18:9-13

My brother is a fisherman; I am not. Well, I'm not much of one. Growing up together, he always caught fish; I struggled. I always thought the fish knew that my heart wasn't in it.

Every now and again I wonder if I am missing out on something great in life and I try fishing again. I think it was Herbert Hoover who once said, "Fishing is much more than fish. It is the great occasion when we may return to the fine simplicity of our forefathers." Statements like this always make me feel guilty. I have four boys. I didn't teach them how to fish. They don't fish. I don't fish. We, then, obviously don't fish together.

My brother still loves to fish. He has one son, and he loves to fish as well. My brother did a great job passing down the love of fishing to the next generation. I admire that.

I don't fish but I do envy those who do and I think I understand what fishermen get out of it. First there is the uncertainty and the hope. Uncertainty about what you are going to catch, if anything. Hope that it will be the big one. There is also the simplicity of it. A boat. A pole. A seat. No TV. No microwave. No sink or stove. No comforts of home. Fishing is not a cruise ship thing. It is just a boat, a pole, a seat and, perhaps, a friend.

Some fishermen go alone, but I think the ones that enjoy it most go with a friend. Often it is the same two fishing buddies who have fished together for years. They have shared adventures—the time the motor wouldn't start in the middle of the lake, or the time the lighting storm almost did them in, or the time they never got the pole in the water because they just talked about meaningful, important things going on in their lives.

Fishing is not about all the bells and whistles of the cruise ship. It is not about big. Two friends in a fishing boat is, well, it's just right. You could squeeze in a third but that third person is just in the way. Two friends. The same two friends returning "to the simplicity of their forefathers."

Most churches in America are not cruise ship churches. Many churches want to be but probably many more don't. They are content to be fishing boat churches.

Fishing boat churches are small. The people have been together a long time. They have a lot of great, shared memories. Many were baptized, married, and will probably be buried in the same church. These small churches do not have all the bells and whistles of a big church, and they like it that way. And they don't go to their church because they like it. Liking or not liking has nothing to do with church. They go because that is what you do. If it doesn't meet all your needs and expectations, well it is not there for your pleasure. It is there because it has always been there.

These small fishing boat churches are hard to kill, but they are dying. Many lost their young families long ago, and once you lose your young families it's really hard to get them back. What young family wants to go to a church that doesn't have other young families? And without young families, the church will inevitably grow old and die out. Churches with a lot of grey hair don't seem to understand that.

Not all fishing boat churches are old. Any church can become a fishing boat church. Back in 2000, I was working for an organization based in Chicago called the Bible League. The goal of the organization was to give Bibles to people all over the world and help those people read them so they would get to know Christ and join His Church. It was and still is a great ministry.

In the winter of 2003, I got a call from my brother,

Jim—not the fisherman brother, Tom, but the brother that I talked about earlier—the one who went to the small outreach church that eventually closed its doors. Jim was now at another church that was planted back in 1993.

At first, this church showed promise. It reached people. It grew. An old grocery store in town was bought and remodeled and the church became known as Pathway Ministries. But trouble soon began. The minister and leadership team were at odds with one another. The ministry teams were each doing their own thing without regard for the others. People started leaving the church. It, like most churches, carried on, but carrying on doesn't always fix things. Finally the minister was asked to leave. Now what?

An interim leader was hired and the search for a new pastor began. That's when my brother called me, but not to fill the pastor position. He called me to lead a married couples retreat. I had just finished writing a Bible study entitled, "How to get the marriage God intended for you," so I was happy to do it. It went well. So well that the couples involved began a campaign to get me to be their next pastor.

I was happy at the Bible League and wasn't really looking for something new. However, the prospect of moving back to my hometown after 20 years appealed to me. My kids never had family nearby and I thought it might be good for them. So, I proposed to Pathway Ministries that I could move from Chicago to Grand Rapids but that I would continue to work at the Bible League during the week. Then on the weekend I would do my best with the church—on a volunteer basis. They thought about it but weren't ready to pull the trigger on such a crazy idea.

The leaders of Pathway pursued other candidates for the open pastor position but the people of the church were so divided they couldn't agree on any particular prospect. Finally, after still more people left the church, the leadership team came back to me and said they were ready to try something different. I should have realized that this was going to be a lot harder than it already sounded. But on a Sunday afternoon, my wife and I loaded up the van with our boys and headed to Grand Rapids, Michigan. None of my kids wanted to go. It was one of those father-knows-best type deals. But did I?

The day after we moved, my wife and I took a long walk in the park and we bawled our eyes out. Were we doing the right thing for our family? For the church?

The first thing I did was take a close look at the membership statistics of the congregation. What I saw wasn't good. The church had 25 kids in the youth group with a full-time youth director. They were the children of the original families that started the church 15 years earlier. But there was the problem: there were hardly any kids younger than that group. I reported to the leadership team that we had only one seventh grader. There were no kids in sixth grade. Only two fifth graders. One fourth grader. No third or second graders. One first grader and two kids in the nursery. The church had lost its young families. How do you get them back?

The next three years were the nightmare of my life. People were mad at each other. People were mad at me. There were power struggles. The church leaders originally wanted me because I was a leader (I had planted two churches, daughtered two churches, started a ministry in Malaysia that had planted over 750 churches), but when I was handed the organizational chart of the church, there were no boxes under my name. I was the leader of one.

So, with my limited power, I did two things:

Bible memorization. The very first service that I led I began with, "Good morning. Welcome to Pathway. Do you think it would be too hard for us to memorize a verse from the Bible every month? Could we do that?" No one said "No." So I said, "How about Romans 12:5: 'We belong to each other and each of us needs all the others.'" Thus, we began memorizing scripture together, reciting them at the beginning of each service.

Daily Bible reading. At the beginning of the New Year, again, at the start of a service, I said, "Good morning. Welcome to Pathway. If you are new here we are trying to memorize a verse every month. You are welcome to join us. Oh, and one more thing, do you think it would be too much to read one chapter of the Bible a day?" No one said, "No." So I made a deal with them. "If you all are willing to read one chapter of the Bible a day, I will be willing to preach out of what you read."

That was it. That was my grand leadership plan. Get people into the Bible and see what happens. In a dysfunctional family when someone steps up to lead, all Hell breaks lose. And that is exactly what happened in my church.

To help keep people accountable and encouraged in

their daily Bible reading, I put up a chart in the back of church so families could keep track of their Bible reading progress. We lost two families over that idea. I also had people leave because they thought memorizing scripture was too much like Sunday school. During the next three years, under my expert leadership, the church went from 120 attendees down to 50.

I began to really question my ability to lead. It didn't make sense. My first church doubled in size during the four years I was there. My church plant in Surrey, BC grew to 500 in five years while daughtering two churches. What was wrong?

Well, if you ask those who left the church they would tell you it was all my fault. I suppose it was—at least to some degree. Another pastor probably could have done things better. On the other hand, in my defense, the church had already lost 180 people before I got there. I learned later that they had also let go of every minister they ever had. Perhaps there was enough blame to go around.

Why am I telling you this story? What does this have to do with fishing boat churches? We tend to think of fishing boat churches as small, traditional, older churches that have been around for a long time. The truth is, a church can get old in one generation. That's what I think happened to Pathway. It started out with young families with passion and energy but somewhere along the way those that started the church just grew old together. They didn't even realize there were no kids in the pipeline after their kids.

The people of Pathway were very close and proud of how friendly they were. But months would go by without a single visitor. I never experienced that with any other church I had led. The church had become a fishing boat church but it still thought of itself as a lifeboat church. The church was filled with good people who loved the Lord, but they had such ownership and pride in their little fishing boat church that no one else could get in.

When I say good people, I mean it. Some of those who left Pathway ended up at a new church plant that has done very well in reaching people. Strange isn't it? The very people that battled against me on every little change are now helping out in a church plant where everything is different. What this tells me is it's not the people that make the difference, it's the context, the perception of the boat. Is this church a fishing boat, a cruise ship, of a lifeboat?

As I mentioned, Pathway went from 120 to 50 people under my excellent leadership. I am so proud and grateful for the 50. They kept the faith. They endured the pain. They believed the vision. They memorized scripture, read their Bibles in their homes, and shared their faith with those around them. Little by little, our lifeboat was filling up. We doubled. We doubled again and again. We have so many families with young children we hardly know what to do with them. We are in danger of becoming a big church.

So, I guess the question is: Can fishing boat churches become lifeboat churches? The answer is "yes," but the cost is high. At this point in my life, I would never want to be involved in revitalizing a church in decline again. The whole revitalization process of Pathway nearly killed me and my family. We spent seven years working twice as hard and enjoying it half as much to accomplish what we did in our church plant in British Columbia in only three years. Planting churches is a lot easier than reviving old ones—even ones that are only

15 years old.

If you Google things like "percentage of churches in decline" or "number of church plants," here is some of what you will find:

- Most churches plateau after 15 years and decline in membership after 35.
- Some 80 to 90 percent of all churches in North America are not growing or are in decline.
- Only two percent of all churches in America are actually reaching truly lost people.
- Churches have a lifespan similar to the typical human being—70 to 100 years.
- Like most human beings, by the time most churches are 15 years old they have reached their maximum size.
- New churches do most of the life saving.

What to do? I don't know. Are fishing boat churches worth the effort to convert to lifeboat churches? It was worth it for Pathway, but I wouldn't want to do it again.

If we are going to try and revitalize fishing boat churches then I propose that we do it together. There has to be a movement. There has to be support. When I did it, I felt alone. Churches around me didn't understand what we are going through. I felt guilty (people were leaving because of me). I felt inadequate (what do I do?). Finally, I felt abandoned (neighboring churches were taking sides depending on the rumors they heard).

If we can't do it together, then maybe we should just cut our losses, plant new churches, and let the old ones die.

Questions:

1. What got your attention in this chapter and what might God be trying to say to you through it?

2. In what ways is your church a fishing boat church?

3. What struggles have you seen in your church between the idea of maintaining traditions versus trying to do more to reach new converts to Christ?

4. Do you think we should spend our effort to change fishermen churches into lifeboat churches or put that effort into planting new churches?

CHAPTER TEN
The "Build It and They Will Come" Attitude

Now the whole world had one language and a common speech. As men moved eastward, they found a plain in Shinar and settled there. They said to each other, "Come, let's make bricks and bake them thoroughly." They used brick instead of stone, and tar for mortar. Then they said, "Come, let us build ourselves a city, with a tower that reaches to the heavens, so that we may make a name for ourselves and not be scattered over the face of the whole earth."

Genesis 11:1-4

A Parable—Part One

I have a story. I'm pretty sure it's not true (since I am making it up). The story is about two rival ship liner companies and two newly discovered, semi-primitive Pacific islands.

The Brightest & Best Ship Company claimed the ship rights for Panay Island. The Try & True Ship Company claimed the rights for Pitcairn Island. Both companies had completely different strategies for getting the ship business happening on each perspective island.

The Brightest & Best Ship Company sent some of their brightest and best people over to Panay Island equipped with complex blueprints for making a ship. There were plans for the ballast system of the ship. There were plans for the electrical system of the ship. There were plans for the interior of the ship. There were plans for the mechanical system of the ship. There were plans for the color scheme of the ship.

Part of the strategy was to find the brightest and best people on the island of Panay and teach them all of these systems in the hopes that they would eventually succeed at shipbuilding. The end result would be a new water transportation system for the people of Panay.

It was hard work. Teaching even the brightest and best people all of the different systems, each with its own set of blueprints, was no small task.

It was a costly operation. Huge investments of time and money were poured into the people and many did not work out. Some candidates started well, but eventually had to be let go because they just couldn't cut it. Prototypes were built but their construction was heavily dependent on the staff of the Brightest & Best Ship Company.

Eventually, a few small ships were built, but they were so expensive that the island could only support a couple of them. And when they broke down, the ships were dependent on the Brightest & Best Ship Company for replacement parts.

In the end, the Brightest & Best Ship Company gave up and left the island. The Panay islanders were left with a few well-trained shipbuilders (at least in their one area of expertise), a few ships, and no way to keep the ship enterprise going. As a result, the people went back to the old way of getting around—on land. But now they were disillusioned with progress and resolved never to push forward again.

For the most part, at least in the United States and Canada, new churches are started (planted), using the Brightest & Best philosophy.

Because church planting is perceived as complicated and difficult, denominations and church leaders usually take the role of the Best & Brightest Ship Company. They go out and try to find the brightest and best from their churches and then train them.

Because training to be a church planter is so complex, most denominations hire out this piece of the puzzle—

often to the most successful mega churches—churches that claim to have grown through outreach and have the big building to prove it.

Just like in ship technology, there are systems to learn and improve upon in church—each with its own tricks of the trade. Demographics. Evangelism. Worship. Music. Rental facilities. Preaching. Educational programs for kids and adults. Small groups. Budgets. Committees. Missional enterprises.

Because the basic blueprint for church planting is so extensive, only the brightest and best, the most talented, and the most gifted dare give it a try.

The cost? Get out a calculator. First there is the investment in formal training for the church planter (in my own case, it was four years of college and four more of seminary). Then there is the salary of the church planter for a year or two. Add to that the monthly expense of rental space, buying chairs, and sound systems. Depending on your marketing plan, thousands of dollars get eaten up by mail, phone, and ad campaigns. The brightest and best church planters today are raising one hundred to two hundred thousand dollars from ever widening sources for their church plants.

With high costs come high expectations. Denominational church planting executives need to sell results to the stockholders (members) of the denomination. Most stockholders are impatient. They want a good, quick return on investment (ROI). This pressure to perform is often passed on to the church planter who must now produce.

Location? Since most church planters are currently pastors in a church or recent graduates, they feel they must move to a new location to plant a church. Having uprooted themselves from networks of people that have taken years to develop, church planters face the challenge of putting down new roots—quickly.

These high expectations lead most church planters down quick-answer trails so common in North America. Their biggest concern becomes: How can I make enough hay (people and money) to fill the barn of self-support?

The most trodden on church planting quick-answer trail is what I call "the draw."

The Draw

I know I am supposed to be talking about ships but I need, for a moment, to talk about baseball. Though baseball is a great game, I have not been to a game in 22 years. It is not that I don't like the game. I used to play—Little League, summer community, high school, etc. But life gets busy. I got married and had four children, all boys.

Now, you would think that with four boys I might just find myself at the old ballpark. But, you see, I have a problem. My four boys like soccer.

Baseball used to be called the national pastime. Everyone played. Young and old, rich and poor. And the best of the best—the crème de la crème—rose to the surface among the baseball ranks. These players attracted thousands of fans to the ballpark, fans who were willing to pay to watch these professionals play. When the fans watched, they were inspired to go back home and play in their own backyards.

Today, baseball is fast becoming a spectator sport. We watch but many of us do not play. This means trouble for professional baseball. If people are not playing baseball in their own backyards like they once did, then the owner of the professional team must attract spectators through other means than just the love of the game. It is now necessary to have a huge stadium, an exciting winning team, a marquee home run hitter, and a great marketing scheme to make it work. As a result we now have bat day, hat day, and bring-your-dog-to-the-park day. Owners are doing all but standing on their heads (some may even be doing this) to pull people in. This is the "draw" —pulling people in. This is what most church planters are forced to attempt. Why?

Denominations raise money to support the brightest and the best church planters who now have a short-term contract. Because this contract of support quickly runs out, most church planters, out of sheer necessity, look for the quickest, easiest way to reach enough people to support them in the game. In this day of mass media, the quickest, easiest way, many believe, is to "draw" or attract them in.

How? By having a winning team. By building an inviting and user-friendly church (stadium). By entertaining the people with great sermons and music. By offering programs to engage both the children and the adults (just like the baseball stadium).

Three problems:

One, there are only a few winning teams. Like baseball, in church planting there are only a few superstars. Most church planters and church plants are average (the average successful church plant has about 120 members in it four years after launching).

Second, drawing people in only works on people that are already attracted to the church (baseball) or at least have some positive memory of it. More and more, people are like my boys—they're busy playing another game.

And finally, this system of church planting leaves

most people in the role of spectator—sitting in the stands watching the professionals play the church planting game. And once people get used to sitting, it is difficult to get them to do anything else.

Okay, I think I have taken more than a moment of your time at the ballpark. Let's go back to Panay Island and the church planting strategy of the Brightest & Best Ship Company. To review, complicated church planting plans force denominations to look for only the brightest and best to go into church planting. High cost and expectations force most church planters into the "draw" strategy. The "draw" is ultimately frustrating for both the church planter and the people the church planter is trying to reach. And in the end, just as on the island of Panay, the people the church planter is trying to reach become disillusioned with the whole process. The church planter, who is tired, eventually quits and goes home.

Questions:
1. What got your attention in this chapter and what might God be trying to say to you through it?
2. Why do you think the "draw" strategy of church planting has been so popular over the last 25 years?
3. What do you like about the draw strategy?
4. What are its limitations?

PART THREE
What Can We Do?

This book has been prompted by the two questions people were asking following the sinking of the *Titanic*: Why weren't there enough lifeboats? Why weren't all the seats filled? These two damning questions led us to a boatload of negative answers. I propose that we now ask a few positive questions. This will perhaps lead us to some positive answers, which, in the end, may lead to some positive action.

- How can we as church members actively get engaged in life saving?
- How do we get cruise ship and fishing boat churches to become lifeboat churches?
- How do we create an environment where every church is always thinking and considering and praying about their next church plant?

CHAPTER ELEVEN
How Can We Build (Plant) More Lifeboat Churches?

They devoted themselves to the apostles' teaching and to fellowship, to the breaking of bread and to prayer...Every day they continued to meet together in the temple courts. They broke bread in their homes and ate together with glad and sincere hearts, praising God and enjoying the favor of all the people. And the Lord added to their number daily those who were being saved.

Acts 2:42,43

A Parable—Part Two

Back to our story about two rival ship liner companies.

As you may remember, the Brightest & Best Ship Company claimed the ship rights for Panay Island. The Try & True Ship Company claimed the rights for Pitcairn Island. We've already looked at the Brightest & Best strategy.

The Try & True Ship Company used a totally different strategy. They sent representatives over to the island of Pitcairn with no plans and no blueprints of any kind. But they did not go empty-handed. They brought a box with a mysterious object inside.

Upon arrival, the people of Pitcairn gathered around the representatives of the Try & True Ship Company and their long, thin, and wide "box." As the company representative carefully lifted the object from its confines, the people strained their necks to see. "What is it?" someone cried. "I can't see!" said another.

"It's a long, thin, wide piece of wood," proclaimed one of the representatives from the ship company as he triumphantly lifted the object high above his head.

Silence. The people hadn't known what to expect, but they somehow expected more. Finally, a small voice from somewhere back in the crowd broke the silence. "What's it for?"

The representative gave a slight chuckle and explained. "Well, there are many uses for a piece of wood…that floats," he said with a twinkle in his eye. "I'm predicting it will change your life. But these uses are for you to discover. This is your island, not mine."

The people appreciated the man's sensitivity to their needs, but they still looked puzzled. So the representative proceeded. "Let me give you a hint. This piece of wood floats and can help you travel on the sea. It will help you move things and people beyond this island, allowing you to explore and interact with people from other islands. It is **true**. Just give it a **try**."

With these words, the representatives from the Try & True Ship Company boarded their ship and headed back to their headquarters.

The people studied the piece of wood. They cut trees down and shaped them into planks to replicate the piece of wood they had been given. Hundreds, thousands were made. Everyone on the island had one. Most had no idea what to do with it.

Some, especially the children, made up games with it. They put it over a log with one kid on each end. They had fun rocking back and forth.

One curious teenager remembered the representative of the Try & True Ship Company went out of his way to mention that the plank of wood floated. So this adventurous teen took one of the planks and used it to ride the waves. Others soon joined in the fun and soon a great wave riding competition was established. His name was Run Jun.

Another bright young woman put two planks together with a box on top to keep the water out. With this water box she could transport materials previously too heavy to carry. It worked so well that others asked her to build a water box for them. The demand was so high that she established The Water Box Company. The cost of transporting materials went down. More people could take advantage of the island market place.

A company called Sail Water Platform Inc. attached a sail as a means of harnessing the wind. Suddenly transportation from one end of the island to the other increased a hundred-fold.

Those living on the rainy side of the island built a little house for the Water Platform. Chairs and beds were added for comfort. Islanders started going farther and farther into the ocean. Inevitably they discovered there were many islands like theirs with many interesting people to meet and new things to learn. Families started taking trips to other islands.

The island was humming with activity. Everyone from great to small was involved at some level. Old stuck-in-the-mud hierarchies of importance based on family and position were rendered obsolete. Every person had a chance to see how far their own talents and gifts could take them.

Representatives of the Try & True Ship Company visited the island periodically. They encouraged the people in their own creativity. On occasion, they gave examples from their own experiences, but for the most part simply cheered the islander's progress.

And indeed the people progressed. Eventually propulsion systems were added. Then cabins and a cargo hold. The platform was expanded to accommodate large groups of people and goods…a ship.

This is a radical new way of thinking about church planting. Or, could it be a radical old way of thinking? Let's put this question on the back burner.

The Try & True approach to church planting does not rely on the talented few, but on the involvement of the average many. It does not rely on large amounts of money, but on the limited resources of the average person. It does not rely on the wisdom of the professional, but on the common sense of the layperson. The Try & True approach to church planting does not begin with complex blueprints for creating a church (ship). It starts with the simple—the "plank."

Just as a ship is nothing but a complicated plank, a church is nothing but a complicated…what? What is church at its simplest form? What is the form of the church that all can and must participate in regardless of talents and gifts?

It is one's personal walk with God. One's intimate, daily talking (prayer) and listening (Bible) to God. The church is just the ship version (more people) of the simple plank—one's walk with God.

You see, just like the people of Pitcairn with their simple piece of wood, everyone can do something with their walk with God. Not everyone does. Many put their walk on the shelf. But many others grab hold of this responsibility and when they do, something happens. When average men and women, young girls and boys, take up the responsibility of talking and listening to God on a daily basis, God shows up. Miracles take place. Average people start doing above-average things.

Two planks and a sail are combined and you have the wonder of a marriage—husband and wife, talking and listening to God and each other, both growing in their relationship with God and each other, sailing their way to unexplored places God has prepared for them.

Next innovation: A large box that floats—a rowboat—one big enough for a family—parents and children, listening and talking to God and each other, all growing in their relationship with God and each other.

Do you see how the simple plank (one's walk with God) begins to expand?

"Hold on," you ask, "how is this even remotely related to church planting?"

Good question. Think back to the island of Pitcairn. In the early stages of the plank one might have asked, "How is a box on a few pieces of wood a ship?" Of course a little, homemade rowboat is not a ship, but it is a step toward it. In fact, isn't a ship just a more complicated form of a rowboat?

Your family may not be a church plant, but it is a step toward it. It may be closer to a church than you think.

Try this experiment: start with the number "1" and keep doubling it (i.e. 1, 2, 4, 8, etc.). It takes just 20 doublings to surpass one million. Now, apply this math to your family. If you are married with two children and your children grow up, get married, and each have two children, and this pattern continues through 20 generations, you will have over one million people in your family tree. What will your spiritual legacy be with these future children?

You see, in a very real sense, you are the pastor of a future church of one million people. What looks like a platform with a box on it today will one day be quite a ship.

So how goes the church plant in your own home?

———

Not only are you planting a church in your future, you are also potentially planting a church in your present. If your family is enjoying the benefits of walking with God each day, why not share your walk with others? If you do, why not support them in a small group? A small group is just a more complicated form of your own personal, marriage, and family walk with God. A small group is more complicated than a plank but not as complicated as a ship. Perhaps it is a pontoon boat.

If you can get one small group going why not try for two, or three, or four?

As you grow, so does the potential of what God can do through you, and soon, despite your low expectations, you will have planted a church.

You start with the simple plank—a walk with God—something average people can and must do. Then people take that plank and share it—first with a spouse if married, then to children if any, and then to other families and individuals. Those that succeed will go on to form a small group. Those that succeed in this step go on to multiply more small groups. Those that succeed at this pull them together in a worship service. Behold, a church has been planted. Those that succeed at planting a church go on to help others do the same.

With the Try & True strategy, everyone is a church planter. The only question that remains unanswered is: how many will be in your church? Two? Five? One small group? Only God knows. You are simply responsible to go as far as the gifts God gives you and the opportunities He places in your life take you.

Perhaps the best thing about this strategy is you don't have to move to a new location. Whoever you are, whatever it is you do for a living, you can begin with this strategy today, right where you currently live. Why uproot yourself and your family? Why not make use of the relationships that you have already formed?

Okay, I left a question unanswered at the beginning of this story. Is this a radical new or old way of thinking about church planting? Well, it is new—in that most church plants are not planted in the Try & True paradigm. But if you go back a few years, it is not new at all.

Most immigrant churches in the New World were started by lay people—families and individuals that brought their faith with them as they moved west. There were no seminaries, no grand denominational plan, and very little support. It was only years later that complexity was added.

And if one goes back even further in history—say to the early church, some 2,000 years ago—it was fishermen and other lay leaders that planted the very first churches. Their training consisted of walking with Jesus for three years.

I began this book asking the question: Why aren't there enough lifeboats/churches? We began this chapter asking the same question in a more positive way: How can we build (plant) more lifeboat churches?

The answer that I have been trying to give in this chapter boils down to this simple thought: Instead of convincing the few, the talented, and the motivated to go out and plant churches, we need to convince the many—the average people who sit in church every Sunday—that they are already involved in church planting in their marriages, their families, and their friendships.

Every group in every church is a potential church plant. Every family that reaches out to a few families is a potential church plant. If we just start thinking this way—then everything every Christian does to live out and extend their faith is potentially the beginning of a new church plant.

Note to denominational leaders: One of the mentors that God has blessed me with in my ministry is Rich DeVos, cofounder of the Amway Corporation. The most significant thing that he ever taught me was this: You reproduce only what you recognize or honor. It is a simple thought. If you give honor to a particular behavior, more people will try to do that particular behavior. What if every church in a denomination considered planting a new church? Can you imagine? It could happen! But the denomination has to start honoring and recognizing what it wants reproduced. And what does it want reproduced? The new church plant. The daughter church. You might think that. But what we really want to reproduce is the mother. Mother churches give birth to church plants. We want that behavior to happen over and over. If we get more mothers, we will get more daughters. Typically denominations give all the honor and recognition to the church plant. The mother goes through the discomfort of pregnancy and birth—losing some of its members to the new church. Why would the typical church that already has enough problems and struggles of its own want to be a mother church?

How about for the honor of it?

Questions:
1. What got your attention in this chapter and what might God be trying to say to you through it?
2. How are you doing in the church plant in your own household?
3. What are you intentionally doing in your household, your family that you believe will be a legacy in the years to come?
4. Why do you think the Try & True strategy of church planting is not as popular as the "draw" strategy?

CHAPTER TWELVE
How Is the Empty Seat Next to You Going to Get Filled?

He told them, "The harvest is plentiful, but the workers are few. Ask the Lord of the harvest, therefore, to send out workers into his harvest field."

Luke 10:2

God's Part

Noah built the boat but God is the one who did the saving. He softens the hearts of those that need saving. He burdens the hearts of those who are saved towards those who need saving.

> *God waited patiently in the days of Noah while the ark was being built. In it only a few people, eight in all, were saved through water, and this water symbolizes baptism that now saves you also—not the removal of dirt from the body but the pledge of a good conscience toward God. It saves you by the resurrection of Jesus Christ.*
>
> 1 Peter 3:20,21

I was only 12 when I made my first sales call. The boy's club at my church had a fundraiser selling light bulbs to help pay for the program. If I sold a certain amount, I could go on the boys campout for free. I wanted to go on the campout; I did not want to sell light bulbs. I was afraid of rejection or what people would think of me, or maybe I was just afraid of people. My father graciously bought some light bulbs from me but then he sent me out on my first sales call...to my grandfather. I know what you are thinking: A sales call to your grandfather? How hard could that be? You have to understand that my grandfather was, or could be: grumpy, scary, and cheap. "How cheap?" you ask. He had a big bag of M&Ms in his fridge. When any of the grandkids came over he would take the bag out of the fridge and give each child two M&Ms. One, two. I kid you not. The bag lasted so long that the M&Ms were stale. So, I didn't want to go to my grandfather's house and try to sell him some light bulbs, but my dad made me go. What I didn't realize was that my father already called my grandfather and the sale was already made. I was going to my grandfather's house just to collect the money.

When I think about sharing my faith with my non-churchgoing neighbors, or my son's agnostic friends, or with some of the guys I play hockey with, I sense a little fear in me. My neighbors might get offended. My son's friends might think his dad is weird. The guys at the rink might, I don't know, reject me somehow, or avoid me.

I think we sometimes believe that we have to save people. We worry that it won't go well. The truth is that Jesus has already paid the price for the salvation we seek to offer. The Holy Spirit is and has already been at work in the lives of those we want saved. The only thing we have to do is respond to the opportunities that God puts before us to share the hope within us.

> *Be wise in the way you act toward outsiders; make the most of every opportunity.*
>
> Colossians 4:5

Our Part

I suppose it comes down to motivation. How are we going to get motivated to actually invite, pull, grab someone—do whatever it takes—to fill the empty seat next to us in the lifeboat called the church?

Good Guilt

I was 19 years old, watching a church service on television. Not really something I was in the habit of doing. On the screen giving his testimony was a young man with cerebral palsy. He had a hard time getting out his words, but this is what I remember him saying: "If someone like me can get up and share his faith, what is stopping you?"

His words motivated me. That week I signed up for a summer mission in Ogden, Utah where I knew I would be forced—helped—to share my faith.

I know guilt can often paralyze instead of motivate. So we often just avoid guilt altogether—especially with regard to our responsibility to share Christ.

Back in Chapter Four, I talked about Lifeboat No. 1—how there were 12 people in a boat that could hold 40. When Lord Duff Gordon was asked if it occurred to him that, if he could get back, he might be able to save the people in the water…do you remember his answer? Here it is: "I have said that I did not consider the possibility—or rather I should put it, the possibility of being able to help anybody never occurred to me at all."

That is one way we deal with the guilt of not sharing Christ with those who need Him—just don't think about it. A better way would be to face it, admit it, and confess it.

Dear Lord Jesus, though you have saved me through no merit of my own, I am often content to sit in my seat on the cruise ship lifeboat with little regard for those still in the water. I confess my lame excuses: I don't have time. I don't know how. I don't dare. I confess to thinking of church as the place that exists to meet my needs. I confess to saying things like, "I work so hard all week with everything I do that when I come to church I just want to relax and reboot, recharge for the next busy week." I confess I have it all backwards. I realize now the only reason you delay in coming back again for the judgment day is that you want people reached who have not yet been reached. That you have called the church to accomplish this task of reaching— that this task is the church's main event. I now realize everything outside of this task in my life is either a distraction or something that can be used to assist in this task. So Lord Jesus, help me see that all the things busying up my life that are not your main mission are really my vacation. And after all my vacationing, help me get to work with the mission of your church.

Thanksgiving

Try being thankful and negative at the same time. Try to give thanks and complain at the same time. It can't be done. When you are busy giving thanks the only thing you can think to do is to give. Giving and thanks go to-gether—that is why it is called thanksgiving.

If you were not raised in the church but someone, somewhere shared their faith with you and it has made all the difference in your life, giving verbal thanks to that person is quite easy. You have probably done it many times. And words of thanks are nice. But if you really want to thank the person who shared his or her faith with you, share your faith with someone who needs it.

If you were raised in the church, if you were born in a lifeboat, giving thanks might not come as readily to you.

The Bible says, "all have sinned and fall short of the glory of God" (Romans 3:16). You can be born and raised in the church but that doesn't mean you don't still

155

need saving. Perhaps a little reflection is all that is needed. Here are some questions that may help you become a bit more thankful:

- When in your life did you feel lost and alone and how did God come along side of you?
- What do you have (gifts, friends, opportunities, purpose, direction, dreams, joy) that God hasn't given you?
- When in your life did your really blow it but God's amazing grace and forgiveness gave you a brand new start?

Counting your blessings (what God has done for you) leads to thanks. Giving thanks makes one motivated to give—of your time, your energy, your enthusiasm, your gifts—to pass on to others what God has done for you.

Inspiration

Charles Lightoller, second officer on the *Titanic*, faithfully helped load the lifeboats, doggedly sticking to the "women and children first" rule (towards the end he had to pull out his gun to push back the men who were rushing one of the few remaining lifeboats). Chief Officer Wilde tried to coax Lightoller to take charge of Collapsible Boat B, but Lightoller simply replied, "Not damn likely." He stayed on the *Titanic* until he was washed off. The suction of a grate on the *Titanic* pulled him under

Charles Lightoller

but a blast of warm air shot him to the surface. Then he saw Collapsible Boat B. It was upside down. Several men had tried to get it off from the deck of the officer's quarters but it fell and landed upside down. Then it was washed overboard by a wave. Once Lightoller was securely standing on the upside down lifeboat, he helped 29 others get on board. For hours he barked out orders on which way to lean to keep everyone on. Finally Lifeboat Nos. 4 and 14 picked them up. Officer Lightoller was the last man to come on board the rescue ship *Carpathia*.

Harold Lowe, 29 years old, fifth officer on the *Titanic*, was in charge of Lifeboat No. 14. He was the only man in charge of a lifeboat that went back to try and save some of the 1,500 people in the water. He tied several boats together, then transferred passengers to free up one of the boats, and then rowed back. But too much time had been spent transferring people, and in the end he rescued only four people (one of those later died). But of all the lifeboats, his was the only one that actually went back to save people.

Harold Lowe

Captain Smith was 62 years old on the maiden voyage of the *Titanic*. He went down with the ship. That's the way it used to be. Francesco Schettino, captain of a cruise ship that went aground off the coast of Italy in late 2011, not only did not go down with the ship, but he was one of the first ones off the ship. We all heard the audio news reports of the Italian coast

Captain Smith

guard ordering him to get back to his ship. He didn't go back. So, I suppose, looking back, Captain Smith did the heroic thing.

Jack Phillips, the chief telegraphic officer coolly and calmly sent the first S.O.S. in recorded history over the new Marconi wireless. "Jack Phillips was a tremendous hero at the time," said curator Alison Patterson. "His messages brought the *Carpathia* to people in the lifeboats and that is

Jack Phillips

the reason they survived." His last message was received three minutes before the *Titanic* disappeared in the Atlantic Ocean. He did not survive.

Joseph Bell

Joseph Bell was the ship's 51-year-old chief engineer. Witnesses said that he and others refused to desert their posts as they battled to keep the electricity going for as long as they could, allowing the ships pumps to keep working and the lights blazing until just minutes before the ship sank.

It was said that 40,000 people lined the route of Wallace Hartley's funeral procession. A newspaper at the time reported that, "the part played by the orchestra on board the *Titanic* in her last dreadful moments will rank among the noblest in the annals of heroism at sea."

Wallace Hartley

Hartley was its leader. We don't know for sure, but many survivors thought the last song played by the band on the listing ship just before the end was "Nearer, My God, to Thee." They played so people wouldn't panic. None of the orchestra members were saved.

Four years after the *Titanic* went down, a young Scotchman, Aguilla Webb, stood up in a meeting in Hamilton, Canada, and said:

"I am a survivor of the *Titanic*.
When I was drifting alone on a spar that awful night, the tide brought John Harper, of Glasgow, also on a piece of wreck near me.
'Man,' he said. 'Are you saved?'
'No,' I said. 'I am not.'
He replied, 'Believe in the Lord Jesus Christ and thou shalt be saved.'

The waves bore him away; but, strange to say brought him back a little later, and he said, 'Are you saved now?'
'No,' I said, 'I cannot honestly say that I am.'
He said again, 'Believe in the Lord Jesus Christ, and thou shalt be saved.'

Shortly after, he went down; and there, alone in the night, and with two miles of water under me, I believed.
I am John Harper's last convert."

In 1912 John Harper was a Baptist preacher from Scotland on his way to lead a crusade at Moody Church in Chicago. He led a crusade in Chicago once before

John Harper with his daughter Nana and niece Miss Leitch.

and everyone was excited to have him again. He left Glasgow for Chicago with his only daughter. His wife died when she was only three years old. When Harper put his little girl in a lifeboat no one would have blamed him if he joined her, being her only parent. But he never considered it. In fact he gave his lifebelt away because he knew that, ultimately, he was already saved. Knowing that he was already saved, he spent his last minutes on this earth trying to save others.

Millvina Dean as a teenager

All these people were heroes. Their stories are inspirational. Their actions saved lives—722 to be exact. On May 31, 2009, Millvina Dean died of pneumonia. She was 97 years old. She was only two months old when she and her family sailed to America on board the Titanic to start a new life. She was the last of the *Titanic* survivors.

Here is my point. All the *Titanic* survivors eventually died. Each had been miraculously saved but, in the end, each died.

I told you about Pastor John Harper. He doesn't sound mainstream, perhaps a bit crazy to most folks—

running around, or I should say, swimming around, trying to convert people. Most books about the *Titanic* don't even mention him. None of the movies include his story. But, it turns out, he really did know what "Are you saved?" meant.

In the movie by James Cameron, the fictional character Rose is telling her story—about when she finally had to emotionally and literally let the man she loved go. She says, "You know there was a man named Jack Dawson, and that *he saved me in every way that a person can be saved.*"

Pastor John Harper understood what the word "saved" meant; I don't think James Cameron did.

Saving people. That is why I got into the ministry. I was pre-med. Some of my friends were pre-med. We sometimes studied and dreamed of our future careers together. But one night I thought about fixing a man's broken leg (I have no idea why this particular thought came to my mind). I remember reasoning that as a doctor I could fix a man's leg but unless he accepts Jesus as His Savior he will still go to Hell (albeit with a nicely mended leg).

I am not against fixing up legs (I am currently recovering from a Achilles' heel rupture that I sustained in the brutally competitive, physical game of badminton—stop laughing; it is not funny). But reaching people for Christ, to be a part of their salvation—that is what I want to do. Not only do I want to, but I get to. I don't have to do it; I get to do it. I get to be used by God to bring ordinary people, people in and about my life, into a relationship with the God who cares so much about them that He sent His only Son to die on the cross for their sins and, who rose again so that when they are saved, it is, unlike the 722, forever. I get to do this!

Thanks Pastor Harper for your passion for those in the water. Your example is an inspiration to us all.

Who are some of the Pastor Harpers in your life? Listen to their stories and be inspired.

Testimony

His name is Rich Francisco. He is a good friend of mine and a brother in the Lord. He is also my chief competitor for the love and attention of my granddaughter, Emma. Rich is the grandfather on the other side. How he got there is quite a story.

Nine years ago, my son, Joe (Emma's father), met the daughter of a single mother who had just started coming to our church. My son eventually married that daughter, and I first met Rich at their wedding—he was dating my son's new mother-in-law. My new daughter-in-law invited Rich to our church. He came. He liked it. But he had a problem. He lived 15 miles away and didn't drive. So do you know what he did? He rode his bike. He didn't drive because he got caught drunk driving a few years before, had his license taken away, and ended up in jail.

In jail, he got into more trouble and was sent to solitary confinement. That is where God got a hold of him. Rich was told that he was not allowed to bring anything with him to solitary. But it wasn't true. One of the inmates pulled Rich aside and told him that there was one item he could request, one item that the guards would have to give him. Any guess what it was?

A Bible. Apparently an inmate cannot be refused a Bible. So, Rich asked for one. And since there was nothing to do in solitary confinement, he read it. The whole thing.

*The word of God is alive and powerful. It is sharper
than the sharpest two-edged sword, cutting between
soul and spirit, between joint and marrow. It ex-
poses our innermost thoughts and desires.*

Hebrews 4:12

When he got out of jail he reconnected with all his
friends, the same friends that had helped him get in jail
in the first place. All except Brenda, the mother of my
son's new wife. She was the one friend that was a positive influence in his life. Rich and Brenda started dating.
My daughter-in-law, Brenda's daughter, invited him to
church, and Rich was saved.

This is Rich's testimony, his story. But let me tell
you what makes his testimony an effective one. First, he
knows what he has been saved from—a purposeless life of
bouncing from one bar and one relationship to another.
Second, he knows what saved him—reading the Word
of God and connecting with others who are reading the
Word (the church).

He knows what he has been saved from and he knows
what saved him. So when he meets someone that looks
like they need saving from a purposeless life, he is motivated to share. To share what? What worked for him—
the Bible and church.

Here is my point. You will never be very motivated
to share God's salvation through Christ unless you know
what you have been saved from and what saved you.
These two things are your unique testimony.

When, in 1975, I went on my first mission experience
to Ogden, Utah, I was taught a very specific way to share
my faith. We were then sent out door to door. We ex-
ecuted what we were taught with various degrees of pro-
ficiency, not without some success. What I learned about

sharing my faith was effective with some people, but it wasn't my story. It wasn't how I got saved. It wasn't what had worked for me. So, ultimately, though it worked, I never got really motivated to work it.

The form of evangelism that you will enthusiastically work at is whatever worked on you. If you were reached by a Billy Graham crusade, you know crusades work and you'll try to get people to attend one. If you were reached by your parents, you know that works and you'll try to tell parents to take responsibility for their children's faith. If you were reached through music…or reading a book… or by listening to a sermon…or by someone carefully explaining Christianity to you…or by experiencing some miracle…whatever it is that worked on you, that is what you will be motivated to share.

Borrowing someone else's story—something that worked for them—may work for you but you will never be that motivated to use it. Salvation is not a cookie cutter thing. God has many different ways to reach many different people. If you want to be passionate about getting people into the lifeboat, you need to figure out how you got there.

For some people like my friend Rich, knowing this is pretty simple. But for others, especially those who grew up in the church, it can be more of a challenge.

My Salvation Story
As I have said before, I grew up in the church. At first my faith was a hand-me-down thing from my parents. But I genuinely believed. Earlier in the book I described to you my teenage problem with grace and doing good and how the story of the Prodigal Son saved me. I got saved from a misunderstanding of grace. When I meet someone struggling with this issue, I go right to the story of the Prodigal

Son. I do it with enthusiasm and purpose. Why? I know it works. It worked for me.

My Other Salvation Story

I became a pastor. My first church, a 70-year-old church, doubled in size and so I got motivated to try out church planting. Off I went to Vancouver to plant a church. It grew and it grew and it grew. But oddly enough, my spirit went the other way. I felt like running away.

My parents had a trailer on the West Coast of Florida where they retreated from the harsh winters of Michigan. I gave them a late night call to inform them I would be arriving the next day.

"Is Marie coming too?" they asked.

"No," I replied. They sensed something was wrong but must have also sensed I didn't want to talk about it. The next day they met me at the Ft. Myers airport. Nothing but silence. The next morning I asked if I could borrow their car.

Tears poured down my face as I headed east across the state of Florida...but I didn't know why. "Why do I feel so empty, so defeated, so dried up?" I tried to stop the flow of tears but the reservoir was seemingly endless. "God, what is happening to me?" I couldn't figure it out, but finally these words found their way past my tightly locked-down consciousness: "This church is killing me."

But how could that be? The church was great. The people were great. They loved me; I loved them. I was being asked to speak at conferences. I was being asked to write articles in Christian magazines. The seminary I graduated from asked me to speak to their church planting class. On the outside all seemed well. On the inside

I was dying.

For two hours I cried as I made my way across the state of Florida. When I hit Miami I just turned south to the Keys. First Key Largo, then Marathon. I just kept driving one road, one bridge, one island at a time until finally the sun went down. Now what? Hotels were $150 a night. No way was I going to pay that, so I did what any sensible Dutch person would do—I looked for the most expensive hotel, parked the car in their parking lot and jumped into the backseat of the car for the evening.

It is not that easy to fall asleep in the backseat of car. Somewhere in the middle of my tossing and turning God spoke to me—as much as God speaks to Christian Reformed people (Reformed people do not typically find themselves on the charismatic side of the Christian shore). And this is what I heard Him say: "I am here." And that was that. Nothing more. I had no idea what it meant.

The next morning with the hot sun on my face I woke up, retraced my trip back to my parents' place, and got on a plane back to Vancouver, back to my home, and back to my church. Strangely, the closer I got to my church the better I felt, though I had no idea why. I kind of felt like Elijah experiencing the silence of God on a lonely mountain. "I am here." It was strangely comforting. The realization that God was with me—God Immanuel—God incarnate—God walking with me—through trouble and confusion. Yes, it was comforting, but it didn't help me know what to do.

That's frustrating, isn't it? You know God is with you and that He cares, but why does He so often delay in showing you what to do? Patience. God is not only a God who is with us, He is also a God who shows us the way—in His time. Over the next three weeks, God revealed to me what "I am here" meant.

This is what I got: "I am here, Steve, and this is what matters: your walk with Me. Not your preaching and teaching and leading and strategizing—simply your walk with Me. Next, I am with you and what matters is your walk with your wife, and together, as husband and wife, your walk with Me. Next, what matters to Me is your walk with your family and your family's walk with Me. And if you, your wife, or your family can help someone else, some other couple, some other family get a walk with Me, well, that is all I want from you."

Wow! I had been trying like crazy to get people into my lifeboat church and the truth was I was barely in it myself. Maybe I was in it, but I didn't have a daily walk with God. I didn't have a daily God walk with my wife or my family either.

So, I started reading the Bible every day. I started praying every day. I kept track of it. I started praying and reading the Bible with my wife and my kids. Guess what we learned? When you start walking with God every day, He shows up. I started seeing that the passage I read for the day was not just some interesting puzzle that might reveal some interesting truth; it was a special word that God had chosen for me to interact with as I went about my day.

It was similar to what I had experienced with my wife. She would tell me something in the morning— usually something that I had heard once before. But, because she said it on a particular morning, it was on my mind. Then things would happen in my day and I would end up relating what she said to what was happening.

So, you can see, in the end not only was I saved from

a misunderstanding of grace back in my college days but now, after my Florida experience, I was saved from dead orthodoxy, from an intellectual only Christianity to a personal, life related relationship with the God of the Bible. I knew what I was saved from and I knew what saved me—reading the Bible and praying with my wife and family every day.

Guess what I am motivated to share? My friend Henry Reyenga and I are working on a book that we've titled *A Walk with God-based Church and the 7 Connections that Can Make it Happen*. Guess what it's about?

I also wrote three Bible studies: *A Walk with God-based Life*, *A Walk with God-based Marriage*, and *A Walk with God-based Family*. Guess what they're about?

I am also trying to live out another book while I write it, entitled, *A Walk with God-based Diet & Exercise Program*.

Where do I get the energy for all of this Walk with God stuff? I will tell you. A walk with God is what saved me. I know it works. And it works with every need that we have. So if I can get someone to walk with God as they tackle a problem in their life (i.e. marriage, family, being overweight and out of shape) I know they will succeed. And when they succeed, they will then be motivated to share their walk with God in that area of need with others.

So, what have you been saved from? And what saved you? Can't think of anything? Start reading the Bible and praying every day and see if God doesn't show up.

Questions:

1. What got your attention in this chapter and what might God be trying to say to you?
2. What makes you nervous or reluctant to share your faith?
3. How might knowing that the Spirit of God has already been at work on the person you seek to share your faith with give you boldness to do it?
4. Does guilt motivate you to share your faith? Does thankfulness? How about the testimonies of others?
5. What is your testimony? What is your salvation story? What have you been saved from? What saved you?

CHAPTER THIRTEEN
How Is the Empty Seat Next to You Going to Get Filled? *continued...*

Let us not give up meeting together, as some are in the habit of doing, but let us encourage one another—and all the more as you see the Day approaching.

Hebrews 10:25

The Church's Part

After I finally understood what God was trying to tell me in the backseat of my parent's car in some parking lot in Florida, I felt like a load had been lifted off me.

I had been planting a church. I had been working hard in the only paradigm of church planting that I knew (build it and they will come = the "draw") where a lot depends on the senior pastor. I had been striving to make sure that the sermon for the coming week was better or at least as good as the week before. Of course I had the help of my wife, family, and the passionate 10 percent of the church that really believed in the vision, but I realized I was slowly burning them out, not to mention myself. I told myself it was for a noble cause; it was for glory of God. Now, I realize that God did not require that my wife, my family, my friends, and I burn out like glorious comets for His purpose and glory. And I didn't have to ignore my family and short-change time with them for time with the church.

With a new sense of purpose and direction, I spoke to my church and told them that I would no longer kill myself to make sure the services were powerfully relevant, finely polished, and entertainingly captivating—not that I had anything against these things. Instead, I was going to take more time with my own walk, my walk with my wife and family. I admitted, however, that I didn't really know what a walk with God looked like and I invited the people of the church to join me in a journey of discovery. Out of 500 attendees, only five families indicated they were interested in this journey.

Undaunted, my family and the five others began a simple talking, listening, repeatedly (every day) walk with God using the Serendipity Bible and homemade prayer sheets (we used ACTS—adoration, confession, thanksgiving, and supplication). The five families began to meet weekly to support one another in this new daily walk. We made a junior version of the prayer sheet so our kids could own their walk, too. Within three months, each of the five families shared what they were doing in their home with others, and what started out as one small group turned into five. A new paradigm of church was at work—a walk with God-based church paradigm.

———————

When the Titanic finally slid out of sight and 1,500 people were calling out for help, every lifeboat had a decision to make. Do we row back and try to save some, or not? There was at least some discussion on each lifeboat. In the end, each lifeboat decided not to row back (Lifeboat No. 14 did go back, but too late).

———————

We often think that the question of whether or not to evangelize is an individual decision. To some degree I suppose it is, and certainly each of us, individually, will be held accountable for what each one does or does not do. But one's individual choice is greatly influenced by the group one sits next to—the church.

So, how excited is your church about evangelism? How excited are you about your church? These two questions are very closely related. If your church is not excited about evangelism, chances are, you won't be either. And if you are not excited about your church, you probably won't be excited about getting people into your church either. So, if you want to get excited about getting people to come to your church (evangelism), you have to first get excited about your church.

How to Get Excited About Your Church

Step One: Join it.

There are so many people these days who belong to a church, but not really. They come when they feel like it. Sometimes they go to other churches just to see what's going on. They think of themselves as very ecumenical. The problem is, from a church leadership point of view, you can't count on them. They are free agents and you never know when they are going to just pick up and leave. It's hard to build a solid team with free agents. And a team is what you need in order to have a successful church—one that members are excited about—one that, ultimately, members get others to join. No, free agents never really commit to your church. So, how hard are they going to work at getting others to get into your lifeboat?

My wife is reading a book with a very interesting title: *Stop dating your church*. You can guess what it is about.

When you join a church, it lets all the other members know that they can count on you. And when you have a whole team of people that can count on each other, it's easy to get excited about your church. And when a team of people is excited about their church, they try to get more people into it.

Step Two: Get involved in it.

Find out what the vision of your church is and do it. If you don't like the vision of your church enough to do it, then why are you in that church? When the church has a spaghetti dinner, go to it. If a ministry in your church needs volunteers, step up. Get involved. Use your gifts. People often like their church in proportion to how involved they are in it. And, again, if people like their church, they are more inclined to invite people to join them there.

Step Three: Give your best to it.

It was the third week of football practice and the assistant coach told me to hang back as a safety valve on a kick off play. So I did. The head coach saw me hanging back, screamed at me, and told me to go take a lap. I had such respect and fear for the head coach that I didn't say anything. I just took my undeserved punishment for the team.

Reflecting on this incident, I realize that a coach must do two things. He must encourage (praise) and challenge (discipline). As fallible human beings, coaches don't always get it right. But the goal of coaching is to create a group of teammates that rely on and bring the best out of each other so that they become more, together, than they could ever be alone. The players, for their part, must give their time, their talent, their effort, and their best. Without the coach doing what he or she does, without the players doing what they are supposed to do, the team will not come together. They will not succeed.

Leading a church is a lot like coaching a sports team. As a pastor, I try to both encourage and challenge. As a fallible human being, I don't always get it right. But my passion and my job is to help create a group of churchmates that rely on and bring the best out of one another so that they become more, together, than they could ever be alone—all for the glory of God. But this will not happen unless the members of my church, for their part, give their time, talent, effort—and their best.

175

There are two things that compete for my church people's best. One is the world and its cares; the other is the "parachurch."

A parachurch is not a church. A parachurch is a Christian organization that specializes in one area of ministry (i.e. youth, education, mission trips, in-depth Bible studies, outreach programs, etc.). The parachurch then attracts members from multiple churches that have gifts and an interest in that specialized area of ministry. These members' time, gifts, and money enable the ministry to succeed.

You see a problem developing here? At least from a pastor's point of view? One of the biggest frustrations that I constantly hear pastors give voice to is that there are not enough people in their churches stepping up into leadership. So when some of their best church members use up most of their time, talent, and enthusiasm outside of the church in a parachurch, well, it can be frustrating.

I do see the attraction of the parachurch from a church member's point of view. You get to be involved in an interdenominational ministry in the area of your gifts and interests. And usually the parachurch ministry is run better than the programs of the church. So it is fun. You are making new Christian friends. You are doing what you like to do. And it is done well.

But again, take a look at it from a pastor's point of view. I am trying lead my church in such a way that there is some excitement among the members for their own church. Remember, if the people of a church are not excited about their own church they will not work that hard at getting new people into it. As a pastor in a church, I don't have the luxury of picking just one ministry and doing it well. I must have a nursery, a youth group, education for all, pastoral care, outreach, and on and on. Unlike the parachurch, I can't skim the cream off the top of the talent bucket of several churches. I am limited to the people the Lord has brought me.

I am not against the parachurch per se. I worked for a great one for six years. It did a ministry that no one church could do. But the sheer volume of parachurches all competing to use the time and talents of the same people needed to run the average church often leaves the church program hurting for lack of the time and talents of its own people.

Parachurches are not going to go away. Any organization that appeals to the special interests of people will always flourish. But everyone involved in a parachurch needs to ask the question we have been considering during this whole section of the book: *How can church people get excited about their own church?* And the reason we're asking this question is because churches reach out to those who "need saving" in direct proportion to their excitement about their own church and what their church does for people.

So, for what it's worth, let me give (from a pastor's point of view) some advice to those considering being involved in a parachurch.

Before you volunteer outside your church, make sure you are volunteering inside your church. If you are already involved in a parachurch organization, figure out how your church can get credit for what you do in the parachurch. If my church gets credit for what my people do through a parachurch, then my people will feel good about what their church is doing. If they feel good about what their church is doing they will be more inclined to try to get more people to come to it.

Here is a practical idea I often share with parachurch leaders. I suggest that they **not** give my church members that are involved in their parachurch ministry a hat and shirt with their logo on it. Instead, I suggest, that they insist the church members involved in their parachurch ministry wear the hat and shirt of their own church. Isn't this reasonable? Why can't the parachurch organization let each local church have its ministry front and center inside of their parachurch ministry? I keep reading in the literature of most parachurches that their goal is to help the church. Well then, I say to the parachurch organizations, HELP THE CHURCH. Help make the church look good. My people are making your ministry look good. Can you return the favor? Help my church members get excited about what their church is doing through your ministry. Because then, maybe, they will also get excited about getting people that need saving in their own lifeboat church.

Step Four: Love and commit yourself to it.

When a commitment made at a wedding ceremony is broken because the couple doesn't like, let alone love, each other anymore, we call it divorce. It happens. But this is not how it's supposed to be. Not to mention the huge wake of pain that washes over everyone connected to the couple.

When people in a church decide they don't like something in their church and quit church altogether, or go to another church, what do we call that?

Normal.

When a person joins a church, I know the commitment made to it is not the same as the commitment made with marriage. But the consequences, the huge wake of pain that washes over everyone connected, feels much like divorce.

As human beings, we are just not good enough to get along in a group without a lot of grace. Grace is another word for love and commitment. We need the love and commitment, the grace of God for each other in the church. A married couple that stays together through tough times because of their love and commitment to each other usually ends up with a stronger relationship. Church members that stay together through tough times because of their love and commitment for each other usually get more excited about their church. And as I keep saying, when church members are excited about their church, they are more likely to get excited about getting others into it.

How to Get a Church Excited About Reaching Those in the Water

I have been trying to figure this one out for 30 years. I think my answer is still a work in progress. So all I can do is humbly share a few observations of what I have learned and a bit of what I am currently trying do as I lead the *Island of Misfit Toys*—the label my church members have given our congregation.[3]

Observation #1: Be done with denial.

There is a good chance your church is not rescuing too many people from the water. According to most research, only two percent of churches are actually doing this. Yes, there are always a few really needy people most churches can point to—people who the church is consuming a lot of energy trying to help. But don't make the mistake of

---

3. This reference is from the movie, *Rudolf the Red-Nosed Reindeer.*

confusing a dependant for a disciple. A disciple is one who does what Jesus did. And what did Jesus do? He made disciples. A disciple makes disciples. If the person who the church is trying to help—trying to disciple—doesn't go on to make disciples, then the church does not have a disciple…it has a dependant.

Be done with denial. I researched my denomination's statistical Yearbook, and learned that it took, on average, 125 church members working an entire year to reach one person. That is 125 members teaching Sunday school, going to evangelism committee meetings, holding outreach services, witnessing to friends, coworkers, and neighbors for an entire year to reach one person.

How is your church really doing?

How is my church doing?

Every year at our church campout we seem to have a few baptisms of people who have never been baptized before. We connect with a lot of people who used to go to church, quit, and are now giving church another try. We also get quite a few people who are like a migratory flock of birds that fly around looking for a church to temporarily land on. Are we really reaching our potential as a lifeboat church?

No, face it, Pastor Steve. Don't sugar coat it. Confess it. Be broken about it. Get angry about it.

Observation #2: Make sure all your own church members are in the boat.

How can your church as a whole get excited about helping others get into the boat if the members themselves are not in the boat?

We tend to see salvation as an individual thing. But isn't a lifeboat rowing back a group effort? In Acts 16 we read about a man who asked, "What must I do to be saved?" That seems like a very individualistic question. The response he got was, "Believe in the Lord Jesus and you will be saved—you and your family" (Acts 16:30,31 NIV). In the Bible, God is always saving a nation, a people.

When I first came to my present church, the folks there were not united; they were not all rowing in the same direction. So we did something so simple and basic that everyone could manage: We talked, and we listened, repeatedly.

Talking: Everyone prayed to God—in their personal lives, in their marriages, their families, and their friendships.

Listening: Everyone was on the same page of the Bible, literally, in their personal lives, in their marriages, their families, and their friendships.

Repeatedly: Everyone was talking and listening with goals and support systems. Our goal with Bible reading was one chapter a day, seven days a week, 365 days a year. To reinforce this reading track, these passages became the study material for our small groups and kids programs. To further reinforce our daily Bible reading, the preaching would come out of the seven chapters that the members read each week. We also would memorize verses of scripture that came out of the readings for the month—we recited them together at the beginning of our Sunday service and helped people memorize them with original songs written by our praise team.

Our goal with all this talking, listening, repeatedly was to make sure every man, woman, and child connected with our church was actually in the lifeboat themselves and that they had something to share—namely their personal walk with God, their marriage walk with God, their family walk with God, and their friendship walk with God.[4]

Observation #3: Move your programs close to the water.
Two years ago we started a program called Pathway Church University.

The tag line reads:
Each one; teach one.

The foundation of our "university" is the belief that every person in our church has been blessed with gifts and experiences that make each person uniquely qualified to teach at least one other person something of value. Since our university began, we have had people teaching doctrine, sewing, guitar, horses, Spanish, book studies, the Bible and its Jewish background, and on and on. The requirement for each course is that there be a learning component, a testing component, and a spiritual component. Because ordinary people are finally teaching something that they know and are excited about, they tend to get more ordinary people to come to the class. Even non-members feel safe taking a class in our church. Our educational program is close to the water—to where the people are—like a lifeboat.

Observation #4: Give everyone a life ring.
Most members in a church have nothing against the idea

---

4. Visit www.path2jesusway.org to listen to my church's scripture songs and learn about our mission statement.

of evangelism. They just don't want to do it or perhaps they don't know where to start. People who talk about it, teach about it, and do it seem to be those few people who actually have the gift to do it. Most church folks do not believe they have the gift of evangelism.

Life rings are placed on boats because, not only are they effective, they are also easy to use. Anyone can pick one up and give it a toss. It is two steps. Pick it up. Give it a toss.

> *Devote yourselves to prayer, being watchful and thankful. And pray for us, too, that God may open a door for our message, so that we may proclaim the mystery of Christ, for which I am in chains.*
>
> Colossians 4:2,3

Pick it up.

Prayer, that is what it means to pick up the life ring. Everyone can pray. The members of our church carry a little prayer card with them 24/7. On that card are the names of people who each member believes would benefit from a walk with God. Every month we bring our cards to church and hold them up before the Lord in our congregational prayer. We have a book in the front of church where people can write the names of those they are thinking about. Our intercessory prayer team prays for these names throughout the month.

Pathway Prayer Card

Colossians 4:-6 *Devote yourselves to prayer ... that God may open a door ... so that we may proclaim the mystery of Christ ...*

Give it a toss.

This step, in the 2-step evangelism process that anyone can do, is a bit more complicated—only a bit more. The purpose of the first step, prayer, according to Colossians 4, is to make us more "watchful and thankful" so that God "may open a door for our message, so that we may proclaim the mystery of Christ." Prayer puts people on our radar and on our hearts. God has a way of honoring our attention to the lost he wants found.

To "give it a toss" means to go through an open door. But, you may be wondering, what is an open door and what do you have to do to go through it? The easiest open door to take advantage of is when the person you are praying for comes up to you and says they want to talk to you about Christianity. If you live your life boldly—living God's way, sharing verses that are speaking to you, praying in public—people will ask, sometimes. But most of the time, an open door is a problem—a problem in the life of the one you are praying for. A family problem, a marriage problem. A problem with health, finances, kids, or work. Usually the problem manifests itself in the form of complaints. If you find someone complaining a lot, it could be an open door.

Okay, so there is an open door. How do you go through it?

Share your faith, your story of how walking with God saved you from whatever problem they are facing. Easy, right?

Yes, it is easy, but most of us won't dare do it. So at our church we use a tract, the size of a business card that simply says, "Walk with God for 6 days and see if He shows up." Inside are six days, each with a verse, a thought, and a question. This is our life ring. This is what we toss. No big deal, anyone can do it. On the back of this tract are these words: "If reading a verse every day was meaningful for you then tell the person who gave you this tract, and he or she will give you a planner with a verse and thought for each day of the whole year."

Observation #5: Celebrate rescues and rescue attempts in your church.

> *So he got up and went to his father. But while he was still a long way off, his father saw him and was filled with compassion for him; he ran to his son, threw his arms around him and kissed him. The son said to him, "Father, I have sinned against heaven and against you. I am no longer worthy to be called your son." But the father said to his servants, "Quick! Bring the best robe and put it on him. Put a ring on his finger and sandals on his feet. Bring the fattened calf and kill it. Let's have a feast and celebrate. For this son of mine was dead and is alive again; he was lost and is found." So they began to celebrate.*
>
> Luke 15:20-24

Once a month, during a Sunday service, our members are offered a chance to light a candle in honor of someone they know who began a walk with God for the first time. It reminds us that we are the "light of the world" (John 5:14).

When someone joins our church, we try to get the people who helped this person get to this milestone to be a part of their joining celebration.

We periodically have contests to see who can invite the most people over to their house during the summer months, or who can hand out the most "Walk with God for 6 days and see if He shows up" tracts, or who can bring the most people to some special event.

We sometimes single out people for special recognition because they have demonstrated extraordinary valor in trying to help others get a walk with God.

The Apostle Paul wrote these words to the lifeboat church at Philippi: "Join with others in following my example, brothers, and take note of those who live according to the pattern we gave you" (Philippians 3:17). That is what we are trying to do. Take note, take notice, of those who are following the example of one of the bravest, boldest lifeboat skippers who ever lived.

Observation #6: Leaders in your church must lead the way.

I have already written how so many of those in charge of a Titanic lifeboat did not lead the way back to the 1,500 men, women, and children struggling in the freezing water. We can blame every person in each lifeboat but the truth is: groups of people do not do anything without someone leading the way. If you are a leader in your church, nothing—in terms of outreach—is going to happen until you and others like you lead the way.

In our church, whatever the initiative is—to read the Bible in our homes, or to memorize scripture, or to invite neighbors and coworkers to church—we always start with the church board. If the church board is not doing it, why should the rest of the church? On the bottom of the agenda for our monthly board meeting we have two permanent items: 1. How is community? 2. Where are the church's next 100 people going to come from?

But why should the board step up and lead if the pastors are not? This is a challenge for me. My gift is coaching, not playing. But the funny thing is, my church folks have a hard time following what I say. They tend only to follow what I say and do. Even God the Father doesn't just tell us what to do. He sent Jesus to show us the way.

One of my outreach goals is to hand out one "Walk with God" tract each day. I put a new one into my billfold every day. I carry my prayer card with the names of people I am praying for and try to look at it, every day.

Maybe you are not a leader in your church. Well, you could be. Just step out and do one thing. Put a tract in your wallet or purse.

Observation #7: Depend on the Lord.

Question: When is it easy to start thinking about depending on the Lord?
Answer: When your life hits an iceberg.

Lawrence Beesely was one of 30 men balancing on the upside down lifeboat, Collapsible Boat B. Because the lifeboat was upside down, we know that everyone on it had been in the freezing water and were now soaked to the bone in the freezing air. It was the middle of the night. They were the middle of the ocean. They had no idea how long they would have to hold on. Do you know what they did? According to Lawrence Beesely, they prayed together —the Lord's Prayer.

It makes sense. When you are in trouble, when you cannot make it on your own, you turn to the Lord, the one who can help.

But the question we have been asking is: How do you get your church excited about reaching those in the water? So the question for Observation #7 is not, how do we get people **in the water** to depend on the Lord? (though that is strangely enough a good question), the question we are really asking is: How do we get the people **in the lifeboat** to start thinking about their need for God?

What? The people in the boat? Why would they need to depend on God? They are in the boat already. You can see the problem.

Maybe those in the boat need to jump in the water. Then they would need God.

I mentioned in this book that for the first 18 years of my life I had never been involved in "saving" someone, and in truth, had never even seen someone else "save" someone. So, I signed up for a mission trip to Odgen, Utah. At the time I knew I was jumping into something that was over my head. I knew that I would not be able to do this on my own. God would have to show up. And He did.

When I was 32, I left the security of a church of 500 and moved to Vancouver to plant a church. I was really worried because I am not an extrovert. My worries proved to be well founded. After two months of church planting I felt alone, discouraged, depressed, like a man lost in a vast, cold, empty sea.

"Lord I need you." That was my prayer. *"I can not do this."*

Over the next year God sent many special people that helped pull me and my new church plant out of the water—the Watkins and the Vanderwouds to name a few. I talked about my neighbor Dave in a previous chapter of this book, the guy I met for the first time on the tennis court. I didn't mention his wife, Collette. She, more than any other at the time, was God saying to me, "I know you can't do it. Just step out in faith because I will supply whatever you lack." Collette was new to church. She was excited about it—for her, her husband, and her sons (It was interesting. They had four boys; we had four boys). She was excited and she was incredibly bold about sharing her excitement. During the first year that she and her family attended the church, she got practically our whole neighborhood to visit our church. She would often say to me, "Hey, if you are out for a walk tonight, stop in. I have a neighbor over. It might be good for you to meet them."

Introverts often know what to say if a person is handed to them on a silver platter. They just don't know how to get them on the platter. What I feared I lacked, God provided.

But He waited for me to put myself into a hopeless situation, one where I would need to depend on Him.

So many of us complain that we don't see the miracles of God in our lives. Perhaps we are not giving God room to work His miracles. If we are not trying anything that requires a miracle of God, why should we expect to see one?

What can your church try or do that will force it to depend on the Lord?

One suggestion: Make some growth goals. "We are

going to reach 50 new people this year." How are you going to do it? One thing's for sure—if you didn't grow much last year, you won't reach 50 new people by doing the same things this year. So what new things are you going to do this year? You don't know? Well, what are you going to do to find out? You probably feel like I'm throwing cold water on you. You are right. If you want to learn to depend on the Lord then you need to get your church into the water.

Perhaps the best way to throw your whole church into the water is to decide to plant a church. Some of your people won't like it. Questions will surface: *How can we plant a church when our own future is not certain? Where will the money come from? How can we afford to lose good people? What is wrong with our church the way it is that we should have to plant a new church?*

You can see, can't you, that you would have to depend on the Lord to face all of this.

What can I say? If your church wants to see God show up, your church needs to step out in faith. One of my favorite stories in the Bible is found in Joshua Chapter 3. There we read that Joshua commands the priests to lead the people of Israel into the Promised Land. They were to take the Ark—God's presence—and step into the Jordan River—the last physical obstacle to the Promised Land—and upon that act of faith God would stop the flow of the water so that the people could walk across on dry land.

The miracle did not precede the faith. That is what we would prefer. *"God, show us your presence and your power and we will step up."* But God's desire is to build faith in us. Faith precedes the miracle. He wants us to step up in faith. Then He will provide the miracle.

I'm diving in, I'm going deep,
in over my head I want to be
Caught in the rush, lost in the flow,
in over my head I want to go
The river's deep, the river's wide,
the river's water is alive
So sink or swim, I'm diving in

Steven Curtis Chapman

Question: What got your attention in this chapter and what might God be trying to say to you through it?

CHAPTER FOURTEEN
The Conclusion

When he saw the crowds, he had compassion on them, because they were harassed and helpless, like sheep without a shepherd.

Matthew 9:36

Senator Smith: Who had charge of the loading of Lifeboat No. 14?

Mr. Lowe: I had.

Senator Smith: And how many people did you put into it?

Mr. Lowe: Fifty-eight.

Senator Smith: And that was when you left the davits?

Mr. Lowe: That was when I left the davits.

Senator Smith: How many people got into that boat after it reached the water, or at any other deck?

Mr. Lowe: None, sir. You see, I chased all of my passengers out of my boat and emptied her into four other boats that I had. I herded five boats all together.

Senator Smith: Yes; what were they?

Mr. Lowe: I was in No. 14. Then I had 10, I had 12, and I had another collapsible, and one other boat the number of which I do not know. I herded them together and roped them—made them all tie up—and of course I had to wait until the yells and shrieks had subsided—for the people to thin

out—and then I deemed it safe for me to go amongst the wreckage...I then went off and I rowed off to the wreckage and around the wreckage and I picked up four people.

Senator Smith: Dead or alive?

Mr. Lowe: Four alive.

Senator Smith: I want to take you back a moment. Before you transferred the 53 people from your lifeboat, No. 14, to other lifeboats…you say you lay off a bit. Where; how far from the *Titanic*?

Mr. Lowe: I lay off from the *Titanic*, as near as I could roughly estimate, about 150 yards, because I wanted to be close enough in order to pick up anybody that came by.

Senator Smith: I understand; but you said you lay off a bit to wait until it quieted down.

Mr. Lowe: Yes.

Senator Smith: Until what quieted down?

Mr. Lowe: Until the drowning people had thinned out.

Senator Smith: You lay off a bit until the drowning people had quieted down?

Mr. Lowe: Yes.

Senator Smith: Then you went out to the scene of the wreck?

Mr. Lowe: Yes

Senator Smith: Had their cries quieted down before you started?

Mr. Lowe: Yes; they had subsided a good deal. It would not have been wise or safe for me to have gone there before, because the whole lot of us would have been swamped and then nobody would have been saved.

Senator Smith: But your boat had, according to your own admission, a water capacity of 65 people?

Mr. Lowe: Yes; but then what are you going to do with a boat of 65 where 1,500 people are drowning.

Senator Smith: You could have saved 15.

Excerpts from the Titanic hearings

Senator Smith thought there were 50 people in Lifeboat No. 14—a boat that could hold 65. Mr. Lowe had said earlier that there were 58 in his boat. So, if we give Mr. Lowe the benefit of the doubt Senator Smith should have said: "You could have saved seven." There were, then, seven empty seats in Lifeboat No. 14.

I think the number seven is a good way to end this book.

Question: Who are the seven people God has specifically placed in your life for you to reach?

END NOTES
True Stories of Panay and Pitcairn Islands

Panay Island, the Philippines

It was the summer of '81—another hot day. But then, for someone from the Midwest, it is always hot in the 8,000 plus islands of the Philippines.

My wife and I were teaching a class on Reformed worship. Seeking to learn what the students may have already known about the subject, we asked them to write out what they thought an order of worship should look like. Most of them wrote out a very specific order—one that came right out of the North American Reformed Church of the 1960s (It was in this decade that my denomination started mission work in the Philippines).

As shocking as this was to us, you will never guess what was first on everyone's order. Now you have to remember this was the hot and humid Philippines where 80 percent of the people played the guitar. The number one item on their order of worship, their thinking on the proper way to begin a worship service was…with an organ prelude.

We had never heard an organ in the churches in the Philippines. But we had never heard a guitar in a worship service either. The students explained that the missionaries of the 1960s brought pump organs to the islands. In the eyes of the missionaries, the guitar was not worshipful enough. But the organs, one by one, broke down and could not be repaired. I later saw one of them—discarded, unused, sitting in some dusty corner of one of the churches.

The upshot was that the people, a culturally musical people, were now singing without instruments in their worship services, holding on to the notion that the proper way to begin a service was with an organ prelude.

So you see, this true story of one mission project on the island of Panay is not unlike what happened in our fictional story about the Brightest & Best Ship Company.

Pitcairn Island

If you get a chance to visit the Big Apple, make sure you stop in at the New York City Museum. I want you to find something once owned by Alexander Smith.

Smith was the sole-surviving European of a bloody showdown between natives of Pitcairn Island and British sailors who landed on the island a decade earlier. It had been a ten-year attempt at creating a tropical heaven that resulted in violence, adultery, and failure.

However, with Smith's survival, the experiment continued. But this time it was different because of something he found, something rescued from the scuttled ship that had originally brought the sailors to Pitcairn Island. It was a Bible.

Smith later said, "When I came to the Life of Jesus my heart began to open like doors swingin' apart. Once I was sure God was a loving and merciful Father to them that repent, it seemed to me I could feel his very presence…and I grew more sure every day of His guiding hand."

Not only did this one Bible change Smith's life but it also changed the lives of the whole island. In fact, when the British Royal Navy finally discovered Pitcairn Island in 1808, they were amazed with the devotion of the people that their report not only made the name Pitcairn a synonym of piety in the nineteenth century, but it also saved Smith from prosecution.

You see, Smith was one of the infamous mutineers on the Bounty—an event made famous in the book and movie *Mutiny on the Bounty*. Along with their leader Fletcher Christian, the mutineers ousted Captain Bligh from leadership and escaped with Tahitian men and women to Pitcairn Island.

Oh, yes, I left you in the New York City Museum looking for something that belonged to Alexander Smith didn't I? You guessed it—the very Bible that turned a dissident and the people of Pitcairn into disciples.

So you see, the true story of the Island of Pitcairn is about a plank (a simple walk inspired by the reading of the Bible) that developed into a Try & True Ship (a community of God).